URBAN HOUSING IN THE 1980s:
MARKETS AND POLICIES

URBAN HOUSING IN THE 1980s:
MARKETS AND POLICIES

Margery Austin Turner
Raymond J. Struyk

The Changing Domestic Priorities Series
John L. Palmer and Isabel V. Sawhill, Editors

┃┇┃ THE URBAN INSTITUTE PRESS · WASHINGTON, D.C.

Copyright © 1984
THE URBAN INSTITUTE
2100 M Street, N.W.
Washington, D.C. 20037

Library of Congress Cataloging in Publication Data

Turner, Margery Austin
  Urban housing in the 1980s.

  (The Changing domestic priorities series)
  Bibliography: p.
  1. Housing policy—United States. 2. Housing—United States. I. Struyk, Raymond J. II. Title. III. Series.
  HD7293.T78   1984   363.5′8′0973   84-21942
  ISBN 0-87766-371-8
  Printed in the United States of America
  9 8 7 6 5 4 3 2 1

BOARD OF TRUSTEES
Carla A. Hills
Chairman
Katharine Graham
Vice Chairman
William Gorham
President
Warren E. Buffett
John J. Byrne
Joseph A. Califano, Jr.
William T. Coleman, Jr.
John M. Deutch
Anthony Downs
Joel L. Fleishman
Philip M. Hawley
Aileen C. Hernandez
Ray L. Hunt
Robert S. McNamara
David O. Maxwell
Lois D. Rice
Elliot L. Richardson
George H. Weyerhaeuser
Mortimer B. Zuckerman

LIFE TRUSTEES
John H. Filer
Eugene G. Fubini
Vernon E. Jordan, Jr.
Edward H. Levi
Bayless A. Manning
Stanley Marcus
Arjay Miller
J. Irwin Miller
Franklin D. Murphy
Herbert E. Scarf
Charles L. Schultze
William W. Scranton
Cyrus R. Vance
James Vorenberg

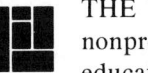

THE URBAN INSTITUTE is a nonprofit policy research and educational organization established in Washington, D.C., in 1968. Its staff investigates the social and economic problems confronting the nation and government policies and programs designed to alleviate such problems. The Institute disseminates significant findings of its research through the publications program of its Press. The Institute has two goals for work in each of its research areas: to help shape thinking about societal problems and efforts to solve them, and to improve government decisions and performance by providing better information and analytic tools.

Through work that ranges from broad conceptual studies to administrative and technical assistance, Institute researchers contribute to the stock of knowledge available to public officials and to private individuals and groups concerned with formulating and implementing more efficient and effective government policy.

Conclusions or opinions expressed in Institute publications are those of the authors and do not necessarily reflect the views of other staff members, officers or trustees of the Institute, advisory groups, or any organizations which provide financial support to the Institute.

The Changing Domestic Priorities Series

Listed below are the titles available, or soon to be available, in the Changing Domestic Priorities Series

Books

THE REAGAN EXPERIMENT
   An Examination of Economic and Social Policies under the Reagan Administration (1982), John L. Palmer and Isabel V. Sawhill, editors
HOUSING ASSISTANCE FOR OLDER AMERICANS
   The Reagan Prescription (1982), James P. Zais, Raymond J. Struyk, and Thomas Thibodeau
MEDICAID IN THE REAGAN ERA
   Federal Policy and State Choices (1982), Randall R. Bovbjerg and John Holahan
WAGE INFLATION
   Prospects for Deceleration (1983), Wayne Vroman
OLDER AMERICANS IN THE REAGAN ERA
   Impacts of Federal Policy Changes (1983), James R. Storey
FEDERAL HOUSING POLICY AT PRESIDENT REAGAN'S MIDTERM
   (1983), Raymond J. Struyk, Neil Mayer, and John A. Tuccillo
STATE AND LOCAL FISCAL RELATIONS IN THE EARLY 1980s
   (1983), Steven D. Gold
THE DEFICIT DILEMMA
   Budget Policy in the Reagan Era (1983), Gregory B. Mills and John L. Palmer
HOUSING FINANCE
   A Changing System in the Reagan Era (1983), John A. Tuccillo with John L. Goodman, Jr.
PUBLIC OPINION DURING THE REAGAN ADMINISTRATION
   National Issues, Private Concerns (1983), John L. Goodman, Jr.
RELIEF OR REFORM?
   Reagan's Regulatory Dilemma (1984), George C. Eads and Michael Fix
THE REAGAN RECORD
   An Assessment of America's Changing Domestic Priorities (1984), John L. Palmer and Isabel V. Sawhill, editors (Ballinger Publishing Co.)

Conference Volumes

THE SOCIAL CONTRACT REVISITED
Aims and Outcomes of President Reagan's Social Welfare Policy (1984), edited by D. Lee Bawden

NATURAL RESOURCES AND THE ENVIRONMENT
The Reagan Approach (1984), edited by Paul R. Portney

FEDERAL BUDGET POLICY IN THE 1980s (1984), edited by Gregory B. Mills and John L. Palmer

THE REAGAN REGULATORY STRATEGY
An Assessment (1984), edited by George C. Eads and Michael Fix

THE LEGACY OF REAGANOMICS
Prospects for Long-term Growth (1984), edited by Charles R. Hulten and Isabel V. Sawhill

THE REAGAN PRESIDENCY AND THE GOVERNING OF AMERICA (1984), edited by Lester M. Salamon and Michael S. Lund

Advisory Board of the Changing Domestic Priorities Project

Martin Anderson, Hoover Institution
John Brademas, President, New York University
Hale Champion, Executive Dean, John F. Kennedy School of Government, Harvard University
Nathan Glazer, Professor of Education and Sociology, Harvard University
Aileen C. Hernandez, Partner, Aileen C. Hernandez Associates
Carla A. Hills, Partner, Latham, Watkins & Hills (Chairman)
Juanita M. Kreps, Economist and former Secretary of Commerce
Thomas G. Moore, Hoover Institution
Richard F. Muth, Professor of Economics, Stanford University
Eleanor Holmes Norton, Professor of Law, Georgetown University
Paul H. O'Neill, Senior Vice President—Planning and Finance, International Paper Company
Peter G. Peterson, Chairman, Peterson, Jacobs and Company
Henry B. Schacht, Chairman, Cummins Engine Co., Inc.
Robert M. Solow, Professor of Economics, Massachusetts Institute of Technology
Herbert Stein, Professor of Economics, University of Virginia; Senior Fellow, American Enterprise Institute
Arnold Weber, President, University of Colorado
Daniel Yankelovich, Chairman, Yankelovich, Skelly and White, Inc.

CONTENTS

Foreword		xiii
Acknowledgments		xv
About the Authors		xvii
1.	INTRODUCTION AND SUMMARY	1
	Years of Change	2
	Sorting Through the Impacts	4
	Highlights	6
2.	METROPOLITAN HOUSING MARKETS	11
	U.S. Metropolitan Areas, 1973–1980	15
	Regional Patterns, 1973–1980	20
	Expected Trends, 1980–1987	28
3.	SIMULATING MARKETS AND POLICIES	29
	Model Households	30
	Model Dwellings	32
	New Construction	32
	Public Policy	33
	Solving the Model	34
4.	ECONOMIC AND POLICY ENVIRONMENT: 1980–1987	35
	Broad Economic Forces	35
	Policy Changes	36

5.	HOUSING IN THE 1980s: ALTERNATIVE SCENARIOS	51
	American Housing in 1987	52
	The Reagan I Program versus the Carter II Program	58
	Concluding Observations	66

Appendix A: The Urban Institute Housing Market Simulation Model: Theory and Solution Process — 69

Appendix B: Generating the Data for Model Solutions — 87

TABLES

1	Northeast and West: Key Housing Market Characteristics	5
2	Summary of Policies for 1980–1987: Reagan I and Carter II Programs	7
3	Highlights of Housing Policy Simulations for Reagan I and Carter II Programs, 1980–1987	9
4	Metropolitan Housing Market Trends for U.S. and Regions, 1973–1980	12
5	Household Composition of U.S. Metropolitan Areas, 1973 and 1980	15
6	U.S. Median Household Incomes, 1980	17
7	Household Composition of Metropolitan Areas by Census Region, 1973 and 1980	22
8	Ratio of Median Income by Census Region to National Median, 1973 and 1980	24
9	Ratio of Net Additions to the Housing Stock to Household Growth by Region, 1973–1980	26
10	Average Vacancy Duration: Metropolitan Areas by Census Region, 1980	26
11	Projected Trends, 1980–1987: Northeast and West Metropolitan Areas	28
12	Projections of National Economic Performance, 1981–1987	37
13	Trends in Assisted Housing Programs Administered by the Department of Housing and Urban Development, 1977–1984	38
14	Simulated Housing Assistance Policies for the Reagan I and Carter II Programs	39

Contents xi

15 Trends in Federal Social Programs by Type of Program, 1965-1988   41
16 Effect of 1981 Changes in Personal Income Taxes, AFDC, and Food Stamps on the Incomes of Families by Income Class   42
17 Federal Personal Income Tax Rate for 1980, Carter II Program and Reagan I Program   44
18 Federal Tax Treatment of Income from Rental Residential Property: Impacts of ERTA   46
19 Northeast: Changes from 1980 to 1987 Under the Reagan I Program   53
20 West: Changes from 1980 to 1987 Under the Reagan I Program   54
21 Northeast: Reagan I versus Carter II Program Outcomes, 1980-1987   60
22 West: Reagan I versus Carter II Program Outcomes, 1980-1987   64

FIGURE

1 Economic Indicators: 1970-1980   14

FOREWORD

This report is part of The Urban Institute's Changing Domestic Priorities project. This project examines the shifts that have occurred in the nation's domestic policies under the Reagan administration and analyzes the effects of these changes on people, places, and institutions.

Housing conditions and costs in the nation's cities are shaped by a vast array of interacting forces, including local market conditions, long-term demographic trends, macroeconomic conditions, and public policies. Sorting through these influences to gain insight into long-term outcomes or to assess the impacts of particular public actions is an intimidating task. Yet it is dangerous to examine individual influences in a vacuum, since interactions between factors often lead to surprising outcomes.

The Urban Institute Housing Market Simulation Model was developed as a tool for comprehensive analysis of housing policies and housing market outcomes. The model provides long-run (seven- to ten-year) forecasts of housing consumption levels and expenditures, given assumptions about initial housing conditions, demographic trends, incomes, input prices, and public policies. These projections refer not only to market averages, but also to individual income classes and demographic groups.

In this monograph Margery Turner and Ray Struyk use The Urban Institute Housing Market Simulation Model to analyze the long-term impacts of Reagan administration policies. Specifically, the Reagan administration's policies with respect to housing assistance, welfare, income taxes, and housing finance are compared to policies that represent a continuation of those pursued by the Carter administration. The outcomes of these two policy scenarios are projected for two dramatically different types of housing markets—one representative of metropolitan areas in the Northeast and one representative of metropolitan areas in the West.

The simulation results focus on how much households spend for housing and on the quality and quantity of housing services they obtain. In addition, market-wide levels of new construction and housing abandonment are projected by the model. These market outcomes provide a basis for anticipating whether urban Americans—rich and poor, black and white, young and old—will be as well housed at the end of the 1980s as they were at the beginning, and whether they will be as well housed under Reagan administration policies as they would have been if the policies of the Carter administration had been continued into the 1980s.

This report is valuable not only for the insights it provides about the likely outcomes of Reagan administration policies under differing market conditions, but also for its discussion of the dynamics of urban housing markets. The long-term implications of public policies cannot be understood without careful analysis of the market context in which these policies operate.

John L. Palmer
Isabel V. Sawhill
Editors
Changing Domestic Priorities Series

ACKNOWLEDGMENTS

The authors wish to thank several people who have contributed to the preparation of this report. Isolde Spiegel and Harold Katsura of The Urban Institute assisted in data collection and computer work. Larry Ozanne provided helpful comments throughout the course of our study. Martin Levine gave us excellent comments and served as our final outside reviewer. The Boeing Computer Services Corporation donated computer time to the study, and financial support was provided by the Ford Foundation and the John D. and Catherine T. MacArthur Foundation.

ABOUT THE AUTHORS

Raymond J. Struyk is director of the Center for International Activities of The Urban Institute. Mr. Struyk is currently involved in a wide range of research projects on urban problems, housing markets, and public policies toward housing. He has served as deputy assistant secretary for research at the Department of Housing and Urban Development. Mr. Struyk is the author of numerous articles and several books in the housing area, including *Housing Vouchers For the Poor: Lessons from a National Experiment*, *A New System for Public Housing*, and *Federal Housing Policy at President Reagan's Midterm*.

Margery Austin Turner is a research associate in the Housing and Community Development Center of The Urban Institute. She has participated in a wide variety of housing market and housing policy analyses. Her recent work includes assessments of specific federal programs as well as broader analyses of the impacts of policy measures on the behavior of homeowners, renters, and real estate investors.

CHAPTER 1

INTRODUCTION AND SUMMARY

The quality and quantity of housing occupied by a nation's families are determined by a complex interaction of forces. Overall economic developments are of paramount importance; but domestic policies that affect the distribution of income, the amount of capital flowing into the housing sector, and the price of inputs (labor, capital, land) also play important roles. Americans are among the best housed populations in the world, a status they greatly enjoy and expect to continue in the future. As evidence of this expectation one need only note the outcry about "homeownership crises" every time mortgage interest rates rise, causing the postponement of the first home purchase of many young families.

Since the start of the Reagan administration, myriad changes in the central determinants of the nation's housing situation have occurred. Many are the direct result of specific administration actions; many are not. Sorting through these changes to identify their net impact on the housing stock and the cost of housing is extremely difficult. Moreover, households, landlords, and developers do not respond instantaneously to various changes. Even among Americans, who are highly mobile, only 20 percent of all households change dwellings each year. Thus, in measuring impacts, it would be best to consider the likely housing situation a few years from now.

The purpose of the analysis reported in this book is to answer two questions about the effects of major changes in domestic policies enacted by the Reagan administration during its first three years in office on how well Americans are housed:

1. Will Americans in urban areas—rich and poor, black and white, young and old—be as well housed at the end of the 1980s as they were at the beginning of that period?
2. Will they be as well housed under the Reagan policies as they would have been under an alternative set of policies more likely to have been implemented by a second Carter administration?

Tackling these questions is a formidable task and one we have approached cautiously. In this chapter we discuss some of the relevant policy changes that occurred from 1981 to 1983, outline our analysis, and summarize the highlights of our findings. The chapters that follow present our methods and results.

Years of Change

Even veteran Washington observers, inured to the massive energy that characterizes the initial months of incoming presidential administrations, had to be impressed by President Reagan's early mastery over the Congress and the scope of the program that was realized. Many of these changes have particularly important implications for the housing sector.

The centrality of the Economic Recovery Tax Act of 1981 (ERTA) requires that we consider it first. The massive income tax cuts for those in the highest income brackets and the minuscule relief for those with incomes below $10,000 are well-known.[1] Given the fact that most households will spend at least some of their incremental income on housing, increased housing demand by those with higher incomes is expected as a result of ERTA. This should be a quite pervasive effect because of the huge number of households affected. In addition, households that receive the greatest tax relief are those that buy new homes, which could raise the overall supply of housing. However, the size of the incremental demand may be somewhat blunted for homeowners because the decrease in their income tax rates as a result of ERTA reduces the value of property tax and mortgage interest deductions.

Other provisions in ERTA increase the profitability of rental properties substantially. If the rental housing market is sufficiently competitive, many of the new tax advantages provided by ERTA will be passed on to tenants, thereby lowering the price of housing for them. This, in turn, should stimulate the demand for rental housing.

Other changes will probably lower housing demand by low-income households, particularly the reductions in disposable income resulting from reductions in benefit levels in the Food Stamp and Aid to Families with Dependent Children (AFDC) programs. Reductions in the benefit levels and number of households who can participate in other social programs that provide in-kind services, such as day care services for children of working mothers, will have the same effect if the services are replaced

---

1. J. Palmer and I.V. Sawhill, *The Reagan Experiment* (Washington, D.C.: The Urban Institute Press, 1982), table 16-7, p. 476.

Introduction and Summary 3

out of disposable income.[2] Nevertheless, it is possible that the housing situation of the poor will not deteriorate, for two reasons. First, the changes just discussed are quite modest for the poor as a group, although some individual households suffer substantial losses. Second, if the demand for new dwellings by higher income households is sufficiently great, the freeing of existing dwellings for occupancy by others might lower housing prices enough to offset the income reductions. This pattern of offsets may be strengthened by the fact that the number of households that suffer income or service cuts is modest compared with the number that gain from the tax cuts.

In addition to these income changes, there have been changes that affect the housing sector more directly. The administration's program in assisted housing will have several impacts. It will shift the profile of those receiving aid to households that are somewhat poorer, and it will cut the aid level across the board by requiring that all participants contribute more of their own income in paying for their housing. Moreover, other benefit reductions are being implemented.[3] These provisions will cause little change in the quality of the housing stock, but they will result in an increase in housing expense burdens. In another change, the administration has shifted the mix of assistance away from supporting new construction and toward giving families certificates to use in renting housing in the open market.[4] This shift is likely to tighten housing markets to some degree. While this may induce inflation in the rental sector, especially in the lower quality portion of the market, it may also result in less abandonment of serviceable housing in the stock.

Mortgage interest rates have probably been the most monitored measure of the health of the housing sector in the past four or five years. Exorbitant interest rates prostrated the home-building industry in 1981 and 1982 and stunned the rate of appreciation of house values that homeowners had come to expect as a matter of course. Less evident but more important over the long term than the roller-coaster ride of interest rates has been action by the Congress and administration that is likely to increase mortgage interest rates permanently in relation to rates on other investments. The massive deregulation of the thrift industry—first on the liability side of the ledger through legislation passed in 1980 and then on the asset side by the

---

2. For a description of these changes, see J. Palmer and I. V. Sawhill, *The Reagan Experiment*, chapters 9, 10, and 12 and J.R. Storey, *Older Americans in the Reagan Era* (Washington, D.C.: The Urban Institute Press, 1983), chapter 3.

3. Fair market rents—the standard used in computing a household's subsidy—have been lowered in the Section 8 existing program.

4. These shifts are detailed in R. Struyk, N. Mayer, and J. Tuccillo, *Federal Housing Policy at President Reagan's Mid-Term* (Washington, D.C.: The Urban Institute Press, 1983), chapter 6.

Garn-St Germain Bill in 1982—removes the housing sector from its favored position in credit markets. The effects on profitability of higher interest rates will have to be weighed against the incentives in ERTA to determine if the development of rental housing that would have occurred in the 1970s is financially feasible in the 1980s.

Sorting Through the Impacts

The foregoing suggests the complexity of determining the net effect of all these changes on particular groups of households. The analysis becomes even more demanding when we recognize that anticipated impacts should vary systematically with conditions in 1980 in different housing markets. The conditions include the vacancy rate, the quality distribution of the stock of dwellings then present, and the income distribution of households as well as the age and racial attributes of household members. Moreover, during the 1980s, the rate of growth in the number of households in an area, changes in incomes, and the cost of building new units will all have powerful effects on the housing circumstances of the population.

Economists typically attack analytic problems of this type by developing a comprehensive model, estimating it for a past period, and then simulating alternative futures. This is the procedure we followed in our analysis. The model we used is the Urban Institute Housing Market Simulation Model, a tool that was initially developed in the early 1970s and since has been improved several times. Over the years it has been used extensively in the analysis of the probable impacts of major shifts in federal housing policies.[5]

The Urban Institute Model analyzes the changes in housing quality and household location in a metropolitan area that occur over a seven- to ten-year period. A model solution provides information on housing consumption and expenditures for homeowners and renters and for different types of households, the upward or downward trajectory of units beginning at different quality levels, and the amount of new construction and housing abandonment in the area. It should be stressed that results are given for various household types, including those that are, in some respects, disadvantaged in the housing market: the poor, minorities, and the elderly. Thus it is possible to go beyond crude overall trends to isolate the changes in the housing circumstances of those groups that in the past have received special attention in federal housing legislation.

As is illustrated in the next chapter, U.S. metropolitan areas are highly diverse in factors that strongly affect the impacts that domestic poli-

---

5. The model is outlined in Chapter 3 and detailed in appendix A.

Introduction and Summary

cies have on the housing market. To capture this diversity while keeping the number of simulations manageable, we elected to apply the Urban Institute Model to composites of the metropolitan areas in two of the four Census regions of the country: the Northeast and the West. Even in the aggregate the metropolises of these two regions differ sharply in several key respects. The parameters of the model have been calibrated for the 1973–1980 period because this is the period for which data were available. Policy simulations must span the same length of time, so our results describe simulated outcomes for 1987. The 1980–1987 period has the advantage of beginning roughly with the start of the Reagan administration and of extending well into the second half of the decade.

Table 1 presents key housing market characteristics of the Northeast and the West. In the Northeast, household growth has been slow in recent years and income gains moderate. Net additions to the housing stock were below the national average but still exceeded the increase in households by close to 10 percent. As a result, markets were sluggish, particularly in the owner-occupied stock. House values and rents rose only moderately, but these increases still exceeded income gains. In the West, by contrast, household growth and income gains were both rapid. The new construction sector responded with a substantial increase in the housing stock, but added units barely kept up with household growth. The resulting tight markets of the West experienced extremely rapid increases in values and rents, which far exceeded income gains. The differences between these regions should provide a guide to much of the range of variation in outcomes that will result from the policies of the Reagan administration, although

TABLE 1

Northeast and West: Key Housing Market Characteristics
(Percentage change, 1973–1980)

	Northeast	*West*
Number of households	4.9	23.3
Median income		
Owners	70.2	81.8
Renters	38.5	49.4
Mortgage interest rate	59.1	59.1
Fuels and utilities index	131.2	100.3
Residential construction index	77.2	88.1
Net additions to housing stock	5.0	22.0
Removals from the housing stock	5.2	3.6
Median house value	74.3	191.1
Median rent	75.5	89.2

the experience of some individual metropolitan areas will be even more striking than that suggested by our results.

Highlights

Before turning to outcomes, we provide a summary of the policy package simulated for the Reagan administration (the Reagan I program) and a hypothetical second Carter administration (the Carter II program) in table 2. These programs are discussed in detail in chapter 4. However, two points should be noted here. One is that these policies are numerous—ranging from income taxes and interest rate policies to housing assistance for low-income households—and can be expected to have pervasive effects on the housing sector. The other is that the two packages of policies are somewhat stylized. The Reagan I policies somewhat overstate the changes actually implemented and reflect what the administration requested in its early budget proposals. The Carter II program is based on our view of what would have happened if Carter had been elected to a second term, not on specific long-term plans formulated in the Carter years.

Over the 1980-1987 period, the Reagan policies lead to a broad improvement in housing quality, thereby continuing the strong postwar trend. Increased housing consumption is driven by increased (nominal) disposable incomes, which effect higher interest rates and higher prices for other inputs than those experienced over the 1973-1980 period. Higher income households experience the greatest improvement and low-income households, the least improvement. The results also show a broad pattern of reduction in the ratio of housing expenditures to permanent income. Homeowners realize the largest reductions. Renters fare less well; indeed in the Northeast, they experience an increase in this ratio, although those in the West enjoy a small decline. In addition, while 22 percent of the 1980 housing stock is withdrawn over the period in the Northeast, no units are withdrawn in the West.

The more interesting results of our analysis are those for the comparison of outcomes under the Reagan I and Carter II programs. Note that while the general macroeconomic environment is the same for both simulations, the huge budget deficit under the Reagan I program causes prices and interest rates to be higher than those in the Carter II economic program. The good news is that the quality of housing occupied by Americans living in urban areas would have improved substantially over the 1980-1987 period, regardless of whether Reagan I or Carter II policies were in effect. On the basis of the results developed here, it is impossible to say that one policy program would have been unequivocally better, either for

Introduction and Summary

TABLE 2

SUMMARY OF POLICIES FOR 1980-1987:
REAGAN I AND CARTER II PROGRAMS

	Reagan I	*Carter II*
Assisted housing		
Additional assisted housing		
Total (units per year)	50,000	250,000
New construction (units per year)	10,000	100,000
Existing (units per year)	40,000	150,000
Tenant contribution rate (as percentage of income)	30	25
Fair market rents (for existing housing)	40th percentile, all units	50th percentile, recent movers
Welfare programs		
AFDC changes in Omnibus Reconciliation Act of 1981	Changes included	No change
Food Stamps, Social Security, Supplemental Security Income	No change	No change
Tax policy		
Personal income taxes, tax schedules	Adoption of ERTA	Indexing beginning 1981
Homeownership rate	No change from 1980	Increase of 2 percentage points
Provisions affecting rental housing	Adoption of ERTA depreciation changes	No change
Macroeconomic effects	5 percent increase in the unit price of housing	No change
Housing finance		
Mortgage interest rate relative to Treasury rates	Increase of 50 basis points	No change

all households on average or for important subgroups of the population. The central reason for this result is the sensitivity of the outcomes to urban housing market conditions. Another reason for the ambiguity is the offsetting effects of policies included in both the Reagan I and Carter II packages.

The overall result is somewhat surprising in light of the massive tax cuts in ERTA. However, the higher mortgage interest rates caused by the budget deficits and banking reforms in the Reagan I program have sharp countervailing effects on the housing sector. These combined influences appear to provide about the same amount of stimulus to the housing sector as the smaller tax relief and somewhat lower interest rates in the Carter II program do. Thus the superiority of one policy package over the other hinges on the structure of local housing markets.

The sensitivity of the findings to key differences in housing markets is illustrated by the figures in table 3, which show the percentage differences in housing consumption and the ratio of housing expenses to income for selected groups of households. Separate figures are provided for the metropolitan Northeast and the metropolitan West. The consumption figures (columns 1 and 2) indicate that in the Northeast, consumption is greater under the Carter II program, while in the West it is greater under the Reagan I program.

Although the causes of these diverse findings are both multifarious and complicated, the essence can be summarized. In the metropolitan Northeast, the principal factor is the higher mortgage interest rates in the Reagan I program as compared with those in the Carter II program, which result primarily from the huge budget deficits but also from deregulation of the thrift industry. The level of new building (in terms of dwelling units) is about 50 percent greater in the Carter II program than it is in the Reagan I program. Thus the market is extremely loose under the Carter II program, and the price of existing housing services is depressed. On the other hand, new units all have the same high price per unit of service, which their moderate-income occupants are paying. The higher interest rates of the Reagan I program make the new construction alternative less attractive to these moderate-income households. A number of those who occupy new units in the Carter II program shift to somewhat larger existing units in the Reagan I program. Moreover, because the level of new construction falls sharply, the overall observed price per unit of service in 1987 is lower under the Reagan I program than it is under the Carter II program.

The explanation for the outcomes in the metropolitan West again has to do with the differences in the pattern of new construction, but diverges sharply from the explanation for outcomes in the Northeast. A key difference between the Northeast and the West in the 1980s is that although under both the Carter II and Reagan I programs there is substantial surplus housing in the Northeast, *no* units are withdrawn in the West under either policy program. Under the Carter II program, the lower interest rates are not sufficient to induce a large number of middle- and high-income households to select new units, as they are able to find existing units suitable to their needs. Consequently, competition for lower quality

TABLE 3

HIGHLIGHTS OF HOUSING POLICY SIMULATIONS FOR REAGAN I
AND CARTER II PROGRAMS, 1980–1987

| | Percentage Difference Between Reagan I and Carter II Programs in Housing Consumption[a] || Housing Expenses to Income Ratio[b] ||||
| | Northeast | West | Northeast || West ||
			Reagan I	Carter II	Reagan I	Carter II
All households	−2.1	4.4	.20	.20	.18	.18
Selected household types						
White, elderly	−3.9	12.6	.26	.30	.22	.22
Black	−5.3	7.0	.23	.25	.24	.22
White, nonelderly husband-wife	−0.9	2.1	.17	.17	.16	.15
Poorest income quintile	−9.0	16.8	.34	.40	.31	.32
Richest income quintile	−0.5	0.0	.16	.16	.14	.14

SOURCE: Tables 21 and 22.

a. Housing consumption is the 1987 level of housing services (per month) provided by the dwelling that the household occupies; it includes structural attributes, housing quality, various amenities, and operating inputs, but it excludes services provided by the neighborhood in which the dwelling is located, such as access to employment sites.

b. Housing expense to income ratio is the average 1980–1987 housing expenditures as a proportion of 1987 permanent or normal income.

units, fueled by household growth, is extremely intense. New construction is concentrated among small rental units.

The Reagan I program produces a different pattern of new construction. In particular, the increase in disposable incomes resulting from the ERTA tax cuts encourages middle- and high-income households to occupy new units, even though the price per unit of services from new units is somewhat higher under the Reagan I program than it is under the Carter II program. This produces about 16 percent more new construction, which is sufficient to relieve the crowding experienced under the Carter II program. This pattern of new construction cools the white-hot competition among the lowest income households and produces the favorable pattern of prices for these households observed under the Reagan I program. At the same time, however, the generally higher prices for inputs, including capital, present under the Reagan I program mean higher housing prices for homeowners and virtually no change in consumption. This leads to equivalent housing expense to income ratios under the Reagan I and Carter II programs.

The following chapters of this book amplify the highlights just reviewed in several ways. Chapter 2 provides an overview of the developments in urban housing over the 1973-1980 period, placing considerable emphasis on regional variations. It also examines the probable course over the 1980s of several factors that strongly affect housing market outcomes, such as the growth in the number and composition of households. Chapter 3 gives an introduction to the Urban Institute Housing Market Simulation Model. Chapter 4 outlines the macroeconomic and policy assumptions embodied in the Reagan I and Carter II packages for the 1980-1987 period. Finally, the results of the simulations for the metropolitan areas of the Northeast and West are presented in chapter 5. The book also includes two appendices. Appendix A provides a detailed and technical description of the Urban Institute Model, and appendix B documents the sources and derivation of the Northeast and West data sets.

CHAPTER 2

METROPOLITAN HOUSING MARKETS

The housing market outcomes upon which our simulation analysis is focused result from the interaction of demand factors, such as household growth, household composition, income levels, and tenure choice, with supply factors, including the price of producing housing services and levels of new construction. In this chapter we examine these factors and the market outcomes they have produced in American metropolitan areas during the 1973-1980 period.[1] National patterns and important variations among regions are identified. In addition, we examine anticipated trends in demand and supply factors for the 1980-1987 period and consider the types of market outcomes that might be expected to evolve. Table 4 summarizes the bulk of the data upon which this discussion is based.

Before we discuss housing market trends from 1973 to 1980, we should consider broader patterns of change that occurred in the national economy over the same period. To some degree, differences between 1973 and 1980 may reflect cyclical patterns rather than ongoing trends. In other words, if the major differences between 1973 and 1980 are primarily attributable to the business cycle, it would be misleading to infer that long-term changes in housing demand and supply occurred over the period.

Separating secular trends from cyclical trends is difficult, but figure 1 displays several indicators that provide a picture of key economic patterns in evidence during the 1970s. This evidence clearly documents one secular shift: the dramatic increases in mortgage interest rates and new home sales prices, not directly related to the cyclical pattern reflected by the unem-

---

1. The period 1973-1980 was selected for examination because it is the longest historical period for which national Annual Housing Survey (AHS) data are available on magnetic tape. As discussed in detail in appendix B, AHS data were used to calibrate the Urban Institute Model's demand and supply parameters and to establish initial-year characteristics for our policy simulations. Our simulations span the period 1980-1987, because the model simulation period must be the same length as the calibration period.

TABLE 4
Metropolitan Housing Market Trends for U.S. and Regions, 1973-1980

	U.S. 1973	U.S. 1980	% change	Northeast 1973	Northeast 1980	% change
Number of households[a]	47,725	54,500	14.3	12,943	13,575	4.9
Husband and wife	30,484	30,880	1.3	8,163	7,565	−7.3
Single head	7,375	11,119	50.8	2,096	2,791	33.2
Single individual	9,866	12,551	27.2	2,684	3,219	19.9
Elderly	8,279	10,186	23.0	2,553	2,926	14.6
Nonelderly	39,446	44,364	12.5	10,390	10,649	2.5
Black	5,436	6,769	24.5	1,252	1,520	21.4
Other	42,289	47,781	12.3	11,691	12,055	3.1
Owners	28,942	33,586	16.0	7,209	7,778	7.9
Renters	18,783	20,964	11.6	5,734	5,794	1.0
Median income						
Owners	$12,700	$22,200	74.8	$13,100	$22,300	70.2
Renters	$7,700	$10,900	41.6	$7,800	$10,800	38.5
Mortgage interest rate[b]	7.95	12.65	59.1	7.95	12.65	59.1
Fuels and utilities index[c]	126.9	278.6	119.5	131.2	303.2	131.2
Residential construction cost index[d]	484.9	884.4	82.4	495.0	876.9	77.2
Net additions to the stock[e]		6,988	13.7		685	5.0
New construction[f]		7,403	14.5		886	6.5
Other additions[g]		2,149	4.2		514	3.8
Removals[h]		2,564	5.0		715	5.2
Vacancy rate[i]						
Owners	1.1	1.4		0.6	1.1	
Renters	5.8	4.9		4.3	3.9	
Median house value[j]	$26,800	$57,700	115.3	$30,700	$53,500	74.3
Median rent[j]	$141	$254	80.1	$143	$251	75.5

a. Number of households: In thousands; U.S. Department of Commerce, Bureau of the Census, *Annual Housing Survey: 1973 and 1980, Part A—General Housing Characteristics for the U.S. and Regions*, (Washington, D.C.: U.S. Government Printing Office), table 1 in sections A through E.

b. Mortgage interest rate: new home mortgage yields (Federal Home Loan Bank Board), *Economic Report of the President* (Washington, D.C.: Government Printing Office, 1981), table 3-65.

c. Fuels and utilities index: Component of the Consumer Price Index for urban consumers, special run requested from the Bureau of Labor Statistics, U.S. Department of Labor.

d. Residential construction cost index: Boeckh Publications, *Boeckh Building Cost Index Numbers*, U.S. Department of Commerce, Bureau of the Census, (Milwaukee, Wisc.: 1973 and 1980).

e. Net additions to the stock: in thousands, difference between total number of housing units, Oct. 1980 and total number of housing units, Oct. 1973; U.S. Department of Commerce, Bureau of the Census, *Annual Housing Survey: 1973 and 1980, Part A—General Housing Characteristics*, table 1 in sections A through E.

Metropolitan Housing Markets

TABLE 4—Continued

North Central			South			West		
1973	1980	% change	1973	1980	% change	1973	1980	% change
12,368	13,680	10.6	12,349	14,884	20.5	10,064	12,411	23.3
7,972	8,013	0.5	8,144	8,537	4.8	6,205	6,785	9.3
1,800	2,632	46.2	1,820	3,067	69.6	1,659	2,609	57.3
2,596	3,035	16.9	2,385	3,280	37.5	2,200	3,017	37.1
2,205	2,506	13.7	1,938	2,662	37.4	1,579	2,093	32.6
10,163	11,174	9.9	10,411	12,222	17.4	8,485	10,318	21.6
1,365	1,640	20.1	2,189	2,764	26.3	628	845	34.6
11,003	12,040	9.4	10,160	12,120	19.3	9,436	11,566	22.6
8,161	9,205	12.8	7,653	9,339	22.0	5,918	7,264	22.7
4,207	4,474	6.3	4,696	5,545	18.1	4,146	5,147	24.1
$12,900	$21,800	69.0	$11,800	$21,000	78.0	$13,200	$24,000	81.8
$7,700	$10,300	33.8	$7,300	$11,000	50.7	$7,700	$11,500	49.4
7.95	12.65	59.1	7.95	12.65	59.1	7.95	12.65	59.1
124.9	268.2	141.7	125.0	265.9	112.8	120.6	241.5	100.3
491.9	895.2	82.0	432.8	792.8	81.9	517.0	972.7	88.1
	1,358	10.4		2,557	19.0		2,388	22.0
	1,528	11.7		2,814	21.0		2,175	20.1
	522	4.0		510	3.8		603	5.6
	692	5.3		767	5.7		390	3.6
1.1	1.2		1.3	1.6		1.2	1.8	
5.9	6.2		7.0	5.3		6.2	4.3	
$25,200	$52,700	109.1	$22,700	$48,900	115.4	$29,100	$84,700	191.1
$139	$239	71.9	$133	$249	87.2	$149	$282	89.2

f. New construction: in thousands; U.S. Department of Commerce, Bureau of the Census, *Characteristics of New Housing: Construction Reports* (Washington, D.C.: U.S. Government Printing Office, 1977 and 1982).

g. Other additions: in thousands; residual of net additions less new construction plus removals; includes publicly owned new construction.

h. Removals: in thousands; U.S. Department of Commerce, Bureau of the Census, *Annual Housing Survey: 1980, Part A—General Housing Characteristics*, table 3 in sections A through E.

i. Vacancy rate: U.S. Department of Commerce, Bureau of the Census, *Annual Housing Survey: 1973 and 1980, Part A—General Housing Characteristics*, table 1 in sections A through E.

j. Median house value and median rent: U.S. Department of Commerce, Bureau of the Census, *Annual Housing Survey: 1973 and 1980, Part A—General Housing Characteristics*, table 1 in sections A through E.

14 URBAN HOUSING IN THE 1980'S: MARKETS AND POLICIES

FIGURE 1. Economic Indicators: 1970–1980

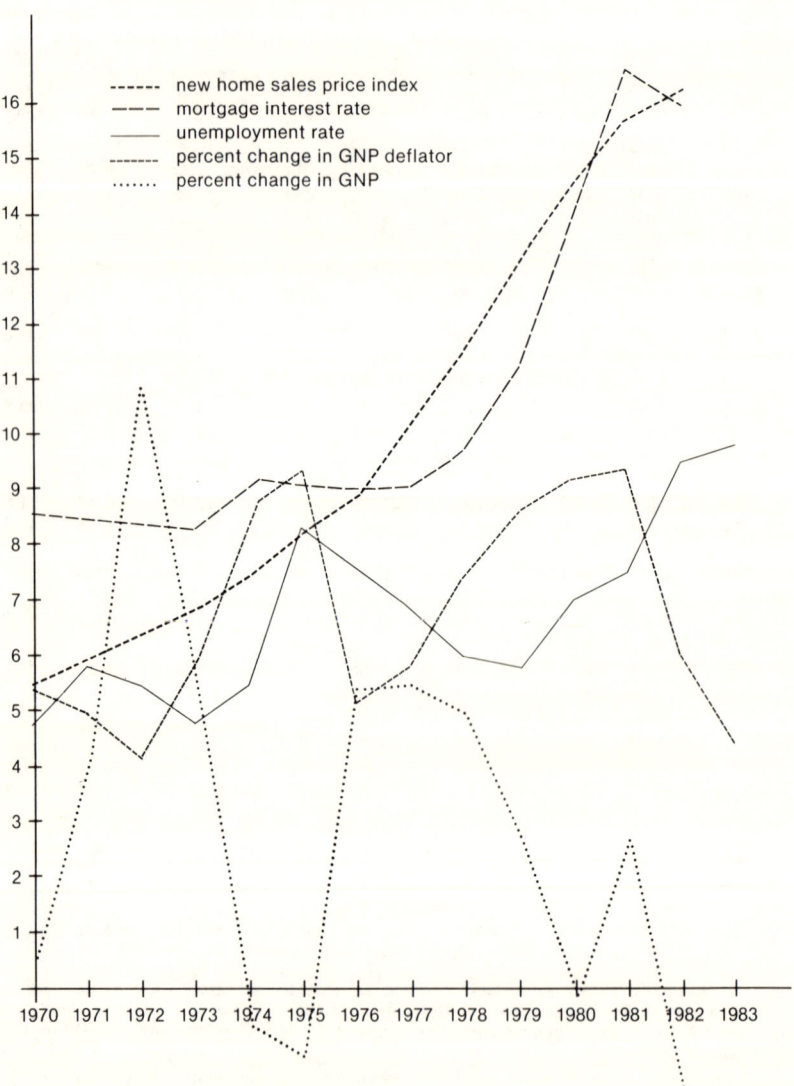

SOURCE: U.S. Department of Commerce, Bureau of the Census, *Statistical Abstract of the United States: 1984*, (Washington, D.C.: U.S. Government Printing Office, 1984).
New home sales price index: table no. 1319, page 739.
Mortgage interest rate: table no. 870, page 522.
Unemployment rate: table no. 669, page 405.
Percent change in GNP deflator: table no. 797, page 485.
Percent change in GNP: table no. 740, page 451.

Metropolitan Housing Markets 15

ployment rate. Thus, capital costs in housing markets undeniably experienced a major upward shift between 1973 and 1980, a trend which has shown no signs of reversal. The remaining indicators traced in figure 1 suggest that, although the years 1973 and 1980 were not at identical points on the business cycle, they were also not at opposite extremes. For example, the unemployment rate was markedly higher in 1980 (7.0 percent) than in 1973 (4.8 percent); but in the intervening years unemployment peaked at 8.3 percent in 1975, and since 1980 has risen even further to 9.8 percent in 1983. Thus one can characterize both years as ones of economic weakness, if not the lowest points in the five-year periods they center.

U.S. Metropolitan Areas, 1973–1980

From 1973 to 1980, the number of households living in American metropolitan areas increased by roughly 14 percent. Behind this aggregate household growth lie significant shifts in the composition of American metropolitan areas. These demographic shifts are important because the composition of metropolitan households in large part determines household incomes and patterns of housing consumption. The most dramatic demographic change is the decline in the proportion of husband-wife households. As table 5 illustrates, in 1973, 64 percent of all metropolitan households were headed by married couples. By 1980 only 57 percent of all households fit this description. Over the 1973–1980 period, the number of single-person households increased 27 percent, and the number of families with a single head increased over 50 percent. Household sizes declined somewhat, but less dramatically than one might expect given observed

TABLE 5

Household Composition of
U.S. Metropolitan Areas, 1973 and 1980
(Percentage of Households)

Household Type	1973	1980
Husband-wife	63.9	56.7
Single head	15.5	20.4
Single individual	20.7	23.0
Elderly	17.3	18.6
Nonelderly	82.7	81.4
Black	11.4	12.4
Other	88.6	87.6

shifts in household composition. The median household size for owners declined from 3.0 persons in 1973 to 2.7 in 1980; for renters, the corresponding figures are 2.1 and 2.0.[2]

In addition to these changes in household size and composition, the share of minority and elderly households increased significantly from 1973 to 1980. Specifically, the number of black households increased by 25 percent—almost double the overall household growth rate—and the number of elderly households increased 23 percent.

Historically, incomes have been comparatively low for all the groups whose representation in metropolitan populations increased during the 1970s. In both 1973 and 1980, incomes of black households, elderly households, single individuals, and households with single heads were all below average. However, some of these groups enjoyed above-average income gains during the 1973-1980 period. Specifically, single individuals and elderly households enjoyed increases in income substantially above the rate for all metropolitan households. Single-headed households as well as black households experienced income increases well below the average for all households.[3]

Thus shifts in the composition of American metropolitan areas were accompanied by considerable variations in the rate of income growth, but not by shifts in the relative income position of the various demographic groups. Table 6 summarizes the distribution of incomes among household groups as of 1980.

The rate of homeownership increased only slightly from 1973 to 1980, from just under 61 percent to just under 62 percent. This small increase is entirely attributable to rising homeownership among elderly and single-person households; rates of owner-occupancy among other population subgroups were essentially constant from 1973 to 1980. The rate of income growth for renters (44.2 percent) was much lower than that for owners (74.8 percent) during the 1973-1980 period. The slow income growth among renters stems primarily from the fact that American households generally become owner-occupants as soon as they can afford to do so. Thus as household incomes rise, people shift from rental status to owner-occupancy, leaving the pool of renters with an increasing proportion of the poorest households.[4] This helps to explain why the rate of homeownership

---

2. U.S. Department of Commerce, Bureau of the Census, *Annual Housing Survey: 1973 and 1980, Part A—General Housing Characteristics* (Washington, D.C.: U.S. Government Printing Office).

3. U.S. Department of Commerce, Bureau of the Census, *Annual Housing Survey: 1973 and 1980, Part C—Financial Characteristics of the Housing Inventory*, table A-1, inside SMSAs.

4. A. Downs, *Rental Housing in the 1980s* (Washington, D.C.: The Brookings Institution, 1983).

TABLE 6

U.S. MEDIAN HOUSEHOLD INCOMES, 1980
(IN 1980 DOLLARS)

Household Type	Income
All households	17,710
Husband-wife	23,180
Single head	
Male	18,775
Female	10,830
Single individual	8,162
Elderly	8,781
Black	10,764

SOURCE: U.S. Department of Commerce, Bureau of the Census, *Money Income of Households, Families, and Persons in the United States: 1980* (Washington, D.C.: Government Printing Office, 1982).

NOTE: These income measures are for all U.S. households, not just those living in metropolitan areas.

has increased among the elderly and among single individuals, since these groups enjoyed disproportionate income gains from 1973 to 1980.

In conjunction with the demand factors outlined earlier, the costs of generating housing services increased substantially in the 1970s. Most notably, from 1973 to 1980, the price of fuels and other utilities rose 120 percent—60 percent faster than the rate of income growth among owners and almost three times as fast as the rate of income growth among renters. Residential construction costs rose slightly more rapidly than did household incomes, and mortgage interest rates also rose substantially—60 percent. One analysis indicates that for a fixed quality of housing services, the overall cost of renting increased 75 percent from 1973 to 1980, whereas the cost of owning increased 114 percent.[5]

Despite the rapid increases in housing production costs relative to household incomes, there was a net addition of approximately 7 million housing units to the metropolitan stock from 1973 to 1980, an increase of almost 14 percent. This net addition resulted from 7.4 million units of new construction, 2.1 million units added to the stock by means other than new construction, and 2.6 million units removed from the stock. New construction was attractive in spite of rapidly rising costs for several reasons. Owner-occupied housing was generally thought of as an excellent invest-

---

5. I. Lowry, "Rental Housing in the 1970s: Searching for the Crisis" (Santa Monica, Calif.: The Rand Corporation, 1982).

ment in the 1970s, and households purchased new units in expectation of substantial appreciation benefits in the not-too-distant future. New rental construction held out a promise of appreciation gains as well as accelerated depreciation deductions and other tax subsidies for real estate investors.

Additions to the housing stock by means other than new construction—primarily conversions from nonresidential uses—played an important role in the 1970s. Annual data on inventory changes suggest that additions other than new construction increase during recessionary periods, when new construction declines, and vice versa.[6] Over 20 percent of all units added to the housing stock in the 1970s were not new construction.

The net number of units added to the housing stock in the 1973-1980 period was slightly higher than the number of new households. Nevertheless, vacancy rates actually declined slightly. Why, if net additions to the housing stock exceeded household growth, did vacancy rates decline? Rydell argues that vacancy rates do not provide good indicators of excess supply, unless they are adjusted by turnover rates.[7] In tight markets, vacancy rates may appear high simply because a large number of units are turning over, whereas in loose markets, unadjusted vacancy rates are low because there is little market activity. In fact, average vacancy duration for units vacant for sale rose substantially during the 1970s, from 5.4 weeks in 1974 to 8.4 weeks in 1980. By contrast, average vacancy duration for rental units actually declined slightly, from 6.3 weeks in 1974 to 5.7 weeks in 1980.[8]

Another way of looking at vacancy rates is to examine the proportion of all vacant units that have been unoccupied for more than six months. Using this measure, we find that long-term vacancies accounted for

---

6. D. McGough, "Additions to the Housing Supply by Means Other Than New Construction" (Washington, D.C.: U.S. Department of Housing and Urban Development, 1983).

7. C. Rydell, *Vacancy Duration and Housing Market Condition* (Santa Monica, Calif.: The Rand Corporation, 1979).

8. Average vacancy durations and annual turnover rates can be calculated using a methodology developed by Rydell (see Rydell, *Vacancy Duration and Housing Market Condition*). Rydell's theoretical proof that the average duration of a housing vacancy equals the ratio of vacancy rate to turnover rate assumes that the pattern of turnovers and vacancy durations is stable from year to year. Seasonal variations in turnover rates make annual averages necessary for empirical work. Rydell's basic methodology was used to estimate the average vacancy duration and annual turnover rate figures presented in this chapter. However, an alternative method was used to calculate the number of units removed from the inventory (which is one component of annual turnover). Turnover rates were estimated from data in *Annual Housing Survey: 1973, 1974, 1979, and 1980, Part A—General Housing Characteristics, U.S. and Regions*: U.S. Department of Commerce, Bureau of the Census, *Current Housing Reports* (Washington, D.C.: U.S. Government Printing Office, 1973, 1974, 1979, 1980), tables 1 and 5 in sections A through E; and *Annual Housing Survey: 1974 and 1980, Part D—Housing Characteristics of Recent Movers, U.S. and Regions.*

roughly 20 percent of all rental vacancies in both 1973 and 1980. The proportion of units vacant for sale that had been unoccupied for more than six months increased substantially over the period—from 35 percent in 1973 to more than 45 percent in 1980. This evidence supports the conclusion that excess production occurred during the 1970s, but strongly suggests that it was the for-sale markets, not the rental markets, that became increasingly glutted.

An examination of the characteristics of units vacant for more than six months yields further insights into housing supply during the 1973-1980 period. Units that have been vacant for more than six months are generally older and smaller and more likely to have plumbing deficiencies than are units that have been vacant only six months or less. Thus a significant proportion of the long-term vacancies are units at the bottom of the housing distribution, possibly bound for eventual removal from the stock. However, newly constructed units also make up a significant share of the long-term vacancies, particularly among units vacant for sale. In 1973, about 21 percent of all the for-sale units that had been vacant for more than six months were newly constructed. In 1980 this measure was about 24 percent, but in the interim it had peaked at more than 45 percent in 1975, providing further evidence of overbuilding and of relatively sluggish markets.[9]

Thus in a period of moderate income growth and rapidly rising costs, the housing sector seems to have overproduced somewhat, particularly for the owner-occupied market. What are the implications of this finding for housing quality and housing expenditures? Metropolitan households generally appear to have enjoyed increases in consumption levels. For example, the size of an average housing unit increased slightly, despite reductions in average household size. In addition, the average age of the housing stock declined, and the number of households living in patently deficient dwellings dropped markedly.[10] Most households also experienced a continuation of long-term declines in overcrowding; the percentage of owner-occupants with more than one person per room decreased from 4.5 in 1973 to 2.8 in 1980, while the percentage of renters with more than one person per room decreased from 6.4 to 6.1. The incidence of overcrowding was consistently higher for minorities and for single-headed households, re-

---

9. U.S. Department of Commerce, Bureau of the Census, *Housing Vacancies: Vacancy Rates and Characteristics of Housing in the United States: Annual Statistics* (Washington, D.C.: U.S. Government Printing Office, 1973 and 1980), table 16.

10. Basic indicators of deficient housing include absence of complete, exclusive bathroom; absence of some or all plumbing facilities; and absence of complete, exclusive kitchen. U.S. Department of Commerce, Bureau of the Census, *Annual Housing Survey: 1973 and 1980, Part A—General Housing Characteristics*, table 1.

gardless of housing tenure, but these groups still enjoyed significant relief from overcrowding during the 1970s.[11]

Given the observed increases in housing consumption and in the costs of generating housing services, one would expect to observe increases in housing expenditures. From 1973 to 1980, the median value of owner-occupied housing rose 115 percent, about 55 percent faster than owners' incomes; interest rates and operating costs rose as well. Meanwhile, median rent rose 80 percent, almost twice as fast as renters' incomes. Thus all households, but particularly renters, spent a larger proportion of their incomes on housing in 1980 than they did in 1973. In fact, the proportion of renter households spending 35 percent or more of their incomes on rent increased from about one-quarter in 1973 to one-third in 1980. Comparable data for owner-occupants are not available for 1973, but the proportion spending 35 percent or more of income on selected housing costs increased from about 8 percent in 1974 to 13 percent in 1980.[12]

In summary, U.S. metropolitan housing markets exhibited five major trends from 1973 to 1980. First, the demographic composition of metropolitan households changed: the share of single individuals and single-headed households increased substantially. Second, by the end of the 1970s, the pool of renters had substantially lower purchasing power than the pool of owners did. Third, the costs of generating housing services increased considerably more rapidly than incomes did, particularly for renters. Nevertheless, owner-occupants and investors in rental housing spurred housing production substantially, so that net additions to the residential stock exceeded household growth and there was an excess of vacant for-sale units. On average, households enjoyed increases in the quantity of housing services consumed, but spent an increasingly large share of their incomes on housing as a result.

Regional Patterns, 1973–1980

The demographic, economic, and housing trends outlined earlier represent averages for the nation as a whole, and although they are interesting

---

11. The definition of overcrowding used here includes those units containing more than one person per room. This standard is more useful than the older rule of thumb, which defined a unit with more than one and one-half persons per room to be crowded. Because crowding has diminished dramatically, it is hard to detect and interpret small year-to-year changes in crowding using the old standard. Furthermore, survey results suggest that the newer standard of adequacy more closely matches people's perceptions of crowded conditions than does the older standard. U.S. Department of Housing and Urban Development, *Housing Our Families* (Washington, D.C.: U.S. Government Printing Office, 1980).

12. U.S. Department of Commerce, Bureau of the Census, *Annual Housing Survey: 1973, 1974, and 1980, Part A—General Housing Characteristics*, table A-2.

Metropolitan Housing Markets

in themselves, they mask some quite significant variations among metropolitan areas. The remainder of this chapter focuses on metropolitan housing in the four Census regions and examines variations in market outcomes in terms of variations in the forces of demand and supply. Of course, in the 1970s there was considerable intraregional variation as well, but by contrasting the four Census regions, we can gain a reasonable picture of major patterns apparent during the 1973-1980 period. After discussing the patterns evident in the 1970s, we present some basic demographic and economic projections for the 1980-1987 period. By considering these projections in light of the 1970s experience, we can begin to hypothesize about likely housing market outcomes for the 1980s.

The most obvious difference between the four regions is in household growth rates. In Northeastern metropolitan areas, the number of households increased only 5 percent; the growth rate in the West was almost 25 percent. This fundamental contrast between slow-growing Northeastern and North Central urban areas and rapidly expanding Southern and Western urban areas dominates all other regional comparisons.

Shifts in the composition of households living in metropolitan areas were apparent in all four regions. The number of husband-wife households grew very slowly, while growth rates for single-headed households, single individuals, elderly households, and black households were above average in all four regions. The group with the largest proportionate increase was consistently single-headed households.

Shifts in population composition were most pronounced in the Northeast, where population growth was slowest. The number of single-headed households increased seven times faster than the overall 5 percent increase, the number of single individuals increased four times faster, the number of elderly households increased three times faster, and the number of black households increased four times faster. The number of husband-wife households actually declined in the Northeast by more than 7 percent. By contrast, growth rates for individual demographic groups in the rapidly growing West were much less variable.

Table 7 highlights the distribution of households across demographic groups for the four Census regions in 1973 and 1980. At the end of the period, a disproportionate number of blacks continued to live in the South, while the share of blacks in the West remained relatively low. A disproportionate number of elderly households continued to live in Northeastern metropolitan areas.

As discussed earlier, the groups whose numbers increased most substantially during the 1970s generally were those with below-average incomes. This helps to explain why, in the Northeast—where household growth was slowest and demographic shifts were most marked—incomes

TABLE 7
HOUSEHOLD COMPOSITION OF
METROPOLITAN AREAS BY CENSUS REGION, 1973 AND 1980
(PERCENTAGE OF HOUSEHOLDS)

	1973				1980			
Household Type	Northeast	North Central	South	West	Northeast	North Central	South	West
Husband-wife	63.1	64.5	65.9	61.7	55.7	58.6	57.4	54.7
Single head	16.2	14.6	14.7	16.5	20.6	19.2	20.6	21.0
Single individual	20.7	21.0	19.3	21.9	23.7	22.2	22.0	24.3
Elderly	19.7	17.8	15.7	15.7	21.6	18.3	17.9	16.9
Nonelderly	80.3	82.2	84.3	84.3	78.4	81.7	82.1	83.1
Black	9.7	11.0	17.7	6.2	11.2	12.0	18.6	6.8
Other	90.3	89.0	82.3	93.8	88.8	88.0	81.4	93.2

increased more slowly than the national average. Income gains were also particularly small in North Central metropolitan areas, where household growth was almost nonexistent among husband-wife households and the numbers of black and single-headed households increased substantially.

Regional variations in income growth rates from 1973 to 1980 resulted in moderate shifts in the relative affluence of the four regions by the end of the period, as shown in table 8, which presents the ratio of each region's median income to the national median. The implications of these figures are sensitive, of course, to variations in the cost of living. The incomes of both owners and renters in the Northeast dropped from above the national average in 1973 to the average in 1980. The incomes of North Central households dropped from about the national average to substantially below the average. In the South, owners' incomes remained somewhat below the national average, while renters' incomes increased from below average to barely above average. In the West, household incomes increased from at or above the national average to substantially above the average. Thus at the end of the 1970s, households in North Central metropolitan areas were the poorest, and households in the West were the richest.

Tenure distributions also exhibited quite variable patterns of change across regions. In the nation as a whole, the number of owner occupants increased slightly more than the overall household growth rate. This pattern was essentially mirrored in North Central and Southern metropolitan areas. However, in the Northeast the number of owner-occupants increased almost eight times faster than the number of renters did, and in the West, the renter population actually increased a bit faster than the owner-occupant population. As of 1980, the rate of owner-occupancy was only 57 percent in the Northeast, 67 percent in the North Central region, 63 percent in the South, and only 59 percent in the West.

In summary, on the demand side, we see a fairly clear picture of slow growth in both population and incomes accompanied by dramatic demographic shifts in Northeastern and North Central metropolitan areas. By contrast, the West and South gained rapidly in both population and incomes and experienced relatively little change in population composition.

How do the four regions compare in terms of the dynamics of housing supply? The input prices of fuels and utilities, which more than doubled nationally, rose most rapidly in the Northeast and North Central regions and somewhat more moderately in the South and West. There was less variation in the cost of new residential construction, but the Northeast experienced the smallest increase while the West experienced the greatest. Thus in Northeastern and North Central metropolitan areas, where population and income growth were slow, utility costs rose astronomically, and construction costs rose more moderately. By contrast, fuel cost increases

TABLE 8
RATIO OF MEDIAN INCOME BY CENSUS REGION TO
NATIONAL MEDIAN, 1973 AND 1980

	1973				1980			
	Northeast	North Central	South	West	Northeast	North Central	South	West
Owners	1.031	1.016	0.929	1.039	1.005	0.982	0.946	1.081
Renters	1.013	1.000	0.948	1.000	0.991	0.945	1.009	1.055

were relatively modest and construction cost increases were most substantial in the rapidly growing, increasingly affluent cities of the South and West. Increases in the cost of fuels and utilities and residential construction consistently outstripped increases in median incomes, particularly among renters and particularly in Northeastern and North Central metropolitan areas.

As one would expect, additions to the housing stock across the four Census regions follow patterns of population and growth. Specifically, Northeastern metropolitan areas experienced only a 5 percent increase in the number of housing units from 1973 to 1980, while the housing stock in the West increased by 22 percent.

As outlined earlier, net additions to the housing stock result from the interplay of new construction, other additions (including subdivisions and conversions), and the removal of units from the active stock. The relative contribution of each of these factors varied markedly across regions. In the Northeast, about 1.4 million units were added to the stock, while about half that number were removed—for a net increase of about 685,000 housing units. Of the 1.4 million housing units added, only about two-thirds were newly constructed. Thus additions to the stock other than new construction played a very significant role in terms of net addition to the housing stock. In contrast, almost 2.8 million housing units were added to the stock in the West, and less than 0.4 million were removed from use. Of the 2.8 million additions, almost 80 percent were newly constructed units. Thus additions to the housing stock in the West reflect a high rate of new construction, few removals, and only a limited number of conversions or subdivisions.

It is interesting that our findings regarding additions to the housing stock in the North Central and Southern regions do not resemble either of the two contrasting patterns identified in the Northeast and West. In both of these regions, the removal rate was relatively high, and an overwhelming majority of units added to the stock were newly constructed, although the number of additions was nearly twice as high in the South as it was in North Central metropolitan areas. Thus in the North Central and Southern regions, a fairly large number of low-quality units dropped out of the stock, the new construction sector was quite active—particularly in the South—and additions from other than new construction were relatively unimportant.

So far we have observed significant regional variations in both demand factors and supply responses over the 1973-1980 period. We now turn to regional differences in market outcomes.

First, how do the housing supply responses in the four regions relate to household growth? As noted earlier, both household growth rates and net additions to the housing stock were lowest in the Northeast and highest in the West. However, the ratio of new housing units to new households varied quite substantially by region, as is illustrated in table 9. In all four regions, the net increase in housing units kept up with the net increase in households. The ratio of new dwellings to new households was highest in the Northeast and lowest in the South and West. Thus excess production seems to have been most evident in the Northeast and North Central regions, where household growth and income gains were slowest.

Given this pattern, one would expect vacancy rates, adjusted for turnover, to be highest in the Northeast and lowest in the West. Indeed, as table 10 shows, average vacancy durations were relatively high in Northeastern and North Central metropolitan areas. In all four regions, vacancy durations were much longer among units vacant for sale than among rental units, and the longest vacancy durations occurred among vacant for-sale units in the Northeast. Data for the latter part of the 1970s also indicate that the proportion of vacant units unoccupied for more than six months was highest in Northeastern and North Central metropolitan areas and well below average in the South and West.

Households in all four regions appear to have enjoyed increases in the quantity and quality of housing consumed. The average size of housing units increased in every region except the Northeast, and the incidence of patently deficient housing conditions declined in all regions. With only one notable exception, the incidence of overcrowding also declined in all

TABLE 9

RATIO OF NET ADDITIONS TO THE HOUSING STOCK
TO HOUSEHOLD GROWTH BY REGION, 1973–1980

Northeast	North Central	South	West
1.08	1.04	1.01	1.01

TABLE 10

AVERAGE VACANCY DURATION:
METROPOLITAN AREAS BY CENSUS REGION, 1980
(IN WEEKS)

	Northeast	North Central	South	West
Owners	9.5	6.7	8.3	8.7
Renters	6.3	6.6	4.9	4.1

NOTE: Average vacancy duration is measured in weeks, and reflects the vacancy rate adjusted by the turnover rate.

regions. The exception to this general trend was the West, where the incidence of overcrowding increased significantly among renters—from 6.9 percent in 1973 to 8.3 percent in 1980. This increase reflects two underlying trends. First, the incidence of overcrowding among Hispanic renters was not only high, but increased dramatically; and second, Hispanic households represented an increasingly large segment of the population in Western metropolitan areas during the 1970s.[13] The increase in crowding among Western households is consistent with the relatively low ratio of added housing units to added households, discussed earlier.

Changes in house values and rents essentially mirror regional growth rates and new construction rates: both values and rents rose most rapidly in the tight markets of the South and West and most slowly in the more sluggish markets of the Northeast. Increases in house values were particularly dramatic in the West, where the median value almost tripled. Rents rose much more moderately than values did in every region except the Northeast, where both rents and values increased by roughly 75 percent. It is interesting to note that while both rents and values rose more rapidly than incomes did in all four regions, the differential was greatest among owners in the West. Despite the substantial income gains enjoyed by Western owner-occupants, the median house value increased 2.4 times faster than the median owner income.

To review, examination of housing market trends by Census regions produces two contrasting scenarios, for which the Northeast and West serve as excellent prototypes. Table 1, in chapter 1, summarizes key characteristics of these two regions. In the Northeast, household growth was slow, population shifts dramatic, and income gains moderate. Net additions to the housing stock were below the national average, but still exceeded the increase in households by close to 10 percent. As a result, markets were sluggish, and a large proportion of vacant units were unoccupied for more than six months, particularly in the owner-occupied stock. House values and rents rose only moderately, but these increases still exceeded income gains. In the West, by contrast, household growth and income gains were both rapid, and population composition changed only moderately. The new construction sector responded with a substantial increase in the housing stock, and added units barely kept up with household growth. Thus only a small proportion of all vacant units were unoccupied for more than six months, and the incidence of overcrowding actually increased

---

13. The high incidence of overcrowding among Hispanics is thought to stem partly from low income levels and a resulting tendency to double up during uncertain economic times, partly from discrimination, and partly from cultural preferences. U.S. Department of Housing and Urban Development, *Housing Our Families* (Washington, D.C.: U.S. Government Printing Office, 1980).

TABLE 11

PROJECTED TRENDS, 1980-1987: NORTHEAST AND WEST METROPOLITAN AREAS
(PERCENTAGE CHANGE)

	Northeast	West
Number of households	4.2	16.4
Median income	74.5	74.9
Mortgage interest rate	8.1	8.1
Fuels and utilities price index	66.9	51.1
Residential construction price index	70.3	80.2

among renters. The relatively tight markets of the West resulted in extremely rapid increases in values and rents, which far exceeded income gains.

Expected Trends, 1980-1987

How can these contrasting scenarios be expected to evolve during the 1980s? Because the Northeast and West Census regions appear to provide good examples of the two contrasting scenarios, we have used them to develop prototype data sets for our simulation analysis. Table 11 presents projected trends in five basic indicators for the Northeast and West in the 1980-1987 period. (Chapter 4 and appendix B describe the sources of these projections in considerable detail.)

Projected population trends suggest that household growth rates will remain low in the Northeast and moderate only slightly in the West. Income gains are expected to accelerate slightly in the Northeast and to stay at past rates in the West. Generally, increases in the cost of fuels and other utilities and residential construction are expected to be more moderate in the 1980s than they were in the 1970s. Mortgage interest rates are expected to climb only slightly from 1980 to 1987. These projections suggest that past rates of housing stock additions will be sustained in the 1980s and that housing markets in the Northeast will remain relatively sluggish, while household growth will continue to keep markets in the West quite tight. Increases in house values and rents should be more moderate in the 1980s than they were in the 1970s, and the ratio of housing expenses to income may actually decline, particularly in the Northeast.

CHAPTER 3

SIMULATING MARKETS AND POLICIES

In chapter 2, we traced some key trends for the 1973-1980 period in housing demand, supply, and market outcomes. These trends—and variations in trends observed across the four Census regions—offer some clues as to what we can expect in the 1980s. However, the workings of metropolitan housing markets are by no means transparent; so it is difficult to sort out the ultimate consequences of expected trends in the determinants of housing demand and supply. Moreover, while the immediate effects of federal housing policies on individual households can be predicted with considerable certainty, it is often far more difficult to anticipate longer term and less direct market ramifications.

The Urban Institute Housing Market Simulation Model was designed to address the difficulties of anticipating the long-term and indirect market effects of housing programs. It incorporates national economic trends, local housing market conditions, and key housing policy initiatives, and it produces meaningful forecasts of supply responses, housing consumption levels, and housing expenditures. The Urban Institute Model was initially developed in the early 1970s and has since undergone several revisions. This chapter provides a nontechnical description of the model's theory and solution process, with an emphasis on mechanisms for simulating federal housing policy initiatives. For a more extensive and technical discussion of the model, with references to previous implementations, see appendix A.

The Urban Institute Model deals with seven- to ten-year changes in housing quality and household location within a metropolitan area. The key phrases of this capsule description are "seven- to ten-year changes," "housing quality," "household location," and "within a metropolitan area." Each serves to distinguish the model from other models or studies, such as short-run explanations of housing market dynamics, location-free theories of the filtering process, and macroeconomic analyses with a national focus.

A metropolitan housing market is represented in the model by 75-100 model households, a comparable number of model dwellings, a building industry, and possibilities for a variety of government restrictions or programs. Thus the key actors in the model are owner-occupant and renter households seeking a place to live, owners of existing dwellings offering housing services at various prices, and a building industry meeting demands at an acceptable rate of return. The behavior of each of these groups of actors can be influenced in a variety of ways by government regulations and subsidies. The model searches until it finds a housing market "solution" by matching households with new or existing dwellings subject to rules of behavior governing each actor. We now consider each of the key actors in turn and then briefly summarize the model solution process.

Model Households

Each model household represents several hundred or thousand actual households; the exact number depends on the size of the metropolitan area to which the model is being applied. A household belongs to one of four household types, determined on the basis of propensity to spend income on housing and on the basis of race, and is characterized by two measures of its income. The household types are white, elderly households; white, nonelderly husband-wife households; other white, nonelderly households, including single individuals and families with a single head; and black households. Each of these household categories is further broken down to distinguish owner-occupants from renters.

The two income measures for each model household are an actual income figure, the estimated mean actual income of the households represented by the model household, and a "model" or "permanent" income figure, a weighted average of actual income and median income of the households in the category to which the household belongs. Although we initially experimented with one "permanent" income figure for each model household, we finally decided that two income figures were necessary. An actual income figure was necessary because certain programs the model is intended to analyze, such as housing assistance payments, operate on actual income rather than on any transformed version of income. However, the assumption of unitary income elasticity embedded in the utility function of the model is inappropriate to measure single-year incomes, so a second, smoothed version of income was required. The model thus uses actual income as the variable directly affected by certain housing and transfer programs, and model income in actually determining the housing location and quality choices that each household makes. A change in actual income (owing to a housing allowance, for example) is of course trans-

Simulating Markets and Policies

lated into a change in model income, but the latter change is smaller than the former.

A household's behavior in the model consists of deciding which of all possible dwellings to occupy, including a new dwelling with any desired level of services—subject to government-imposed minimum standards for new construction—or any of the existing dwellings in the model. The household makes its decision on the basis of the price and quantity of housing services offered by each dwelling, assuming that micro-equilibrium conditions apply so that the quantity of services forthcoming from a dwelling is equal to the quantity of services demanded by the household at that price.

The micro-equilibrium combination of price and quantity for a particular model household in a particular model dwelling is complicated somewhat by the fact that the net price actually incurred by the household may differ from the gross price realized by the producer. A primary example of such a difference arises in the case of owner-occupants who itemize their federal income tax deductions. For these households, mortgage interest and property tax deductions significantly reduce the net price of housing services. In addition, the net price incurred by all owner-occupants is reduced by appreciation benefits. Finally, landlords are assumed to pass on to renter households a portion of the tax benefits they obtain from accelerated depreciation deductions.

A key determinant of the housing consumption decision is a household's preference for housing relative to other goods. Preferences are assumed to vary by household type and tenure, but also by model income. Thus within a given type and tenure grouping, poor households are willing to commit a larger proportion of after-tax income to housing than are richer households. Richer households naturally spend considerably more for their housing than do poor households, but not as much as if all households had the same preference for housing relative to other goods.

Households also consider three characteristics of the zone in which a dwelling is located. Central city locations are differentiated from the suburbs, and the three zonal characteristics of relevance are average travel time to and from work, relative wealth (measured by the average net rent per dwelling), and—for white households only—the racial composition of the zone. Travel time is simply introduced into the model as a piece of exogenous information about each zone. Zonal wealth and racial composition are determined by the model itself, with the result that there is a two-way interaction between household choice and the zonal characteristics. All the variables that influence household choices are combined in a utility function that the household is attempting to maximize. Thus a model household is assumed to determine how much utility it would derive from each of the existing model dwellings and from a new dwelling, and to rank all dwellings in terms of their utility.

Model Dwellings

Each model dwelling, like each model household, represents several hundred or thousand actual cases; in fact, the number of actual cases represented by a model unit is, apart from minor statistical adjustments, the same as the number of cases represented by a model household. Each model dwelling belongs to one of two zones, central city or suburb, that differ in accessibility, initial wealth, and initial racial composition. Each model dwelling is also characterized by the quantity of housing services supplied, a flow of output per month, at the beginning of the period to which the model applies. The quantity of housing services a dwelling supplies, one of the basic concepts of the model, refers to an index of all the things of value that a physical structure provides, including space, shelter, privacy, and a pleasing design. It does not refer to the neighborhood characteristics associated with each dwelling; these are measured by the various attributes of the zone in which a dwelling is located.

The behavior of the owners of existing dwellings, whether they are landlords or owner-occupant households, consists of making price-quantity offers with the goal of maximizing expected profits. Each price-quantity offer consists of a quantity of housing services to be provided at the end of the period to which the model refers and a price at which that quantity will be provided. Price-quantity offers for each dwelling must lie along a supply curve whose position depends on the initial quantity of housing services offered by the dwelling and two parameters of the model, one related to a real depreciation rate and the other to an elasticity of supply with respect to price. These two parameters determine the supply elasticity of the existing housing stock. As indicated earlier, the particular price-quantity combination offered to a particular household by the owner of a particular dwelling is set at the intersection of the dwelling's supply curve and the household's demand curve, assuming micro-equilibrium conditions.

The model includes a minimum price per unit of housing service, defined as the price that is just sufficient to cover the cost of operating a dwelling. If the owner of a dwelling is unable to find an occupant at any price at or above this minimum, then the owner withdraws the dwelling from the stock of housing. Withdrawal can take the form of long-term vacancy, demolition, conversion to nonresidential use, or abandonment. The model does not distinguish among these different kinds of withdrawal.

New Construction

The third actor in the model, the building industry, plays a more passive role than do model dwellings. The industry is characterized by a hori-

Simulating Markets and Policies

zontal supply curve; that is, it is prepared to offer new dwellings at a monthly total cost that is proportional to the level of services the dwelling provides. The price per unit of service at which new dwellings are available is established outside the model on the basis of data for each housing market.

For a time span much shorter than seven to ten years the assumption of a perfectly elastic supply of new housing would be inappropriate. The mortgage market and building supply industries are subject to capacity limitations, which sometimes strongly influence the course of new construction in the short run. Even over a ten-year span, the supply of land is limited, and the effect is to make the supply of new housing less than perfectly elastic. Muth has argued convincingly, however, that the increase in land prices owing to residential users' bidding away of land from other users has only a negligible effect on the long-run supply elasticity of new housing.[1]

Public Policy

Public policies can intervene to influence the behavior of actors at several junctures in the model. Specifically, in the model framework, activities of the public sector operate in five major ways.

1. Policies can alter households' disposable incomes, for example, by means of taxes, welfare payments, or housing allowances.
2. Public policies can affect the costs of producing housing services. The most common example of policies with this kind of impact are those that affect mortgage interest rates.
3. The public sector can alter the effective price incurred by housing consumers; the most notable example of this is the price subsidy provided by mortgage interest and property tax deductions from federal income taxes.
4. The public sector can intervene by means of the direct provision of publicly owned or subsidized housing units. Policies of this type are simulated by simply removing the affected households from the market solution and allocating them to exogenously provided dwellings.
5. The public sector can constrain housing choices, for example, by setting minimum quality standards for new construction or by imposing conditions on the receipt of income transfers.

---

1. Muth, R. and Wetzler, E., "Effects of Constraints on Single-Unit Housing Costs" (Arlington, Virginia: Institute for Defense Analysis, 1968).

Thus the Urban Institute Model makes it possible to simulate the impacts of a wide range of public policies, either individually or in combination.

Solving the Model

A model solution is characterized by three basic conditions. First, each household is consuming the quantity of housing services and paying the unit price that represents the intersection of household demand and dwelling supply. Second, each household occupies the dwelling in which it obtains the highest utility, given the established market prices. In other words, a household may not necessarily be assigned to the dwelling it most prefers, but all dwellings that offer greater utility than the dwelling to which the household has been assigned are occupied by households that pay higher unit prices. Third, the neighborhood conditions, racial composition and relative wealth, generated by the assignment of model households to model dwellings must correspond to the assumed conditions upon which the assignment was based.

The first condition for the model solution is satisfied by only allowing households to evaluate the utility offered by dwellings at the intersection of household demand and dwelling supply. Thus no other price-quantity combinations are ever considered. Once each household has ranked all available dwellings, including a new dwelling, in order of utility, households are assigned one at a time to their preferred dwellings and reassigned only when a subsequent household is willing to pay a higher unit price for an allocated dwelling. After all households have been assigned—and reassigned—in this manner, the second condition for the solution is satisfied.

Satisfying the third condition for the model solution generally involves multiple attempts at assigning households to dwellings. Specifically, the utility derived by a household from a particular dwelling depends upon the racial composition and relative wealth of the zone in which that dwelling is located. Thus the solution process must begin with assumptions about the characteristics of each zone. However, when all the households have been assigned to dwellings, the resulting zonal characteristics may differ from the assumptions upon which the assignment was based. If such differences occur, the original assumptions about zonal characteristics are replaced with the results of the first assignment. Then household utilities are recalculated for each dwelling, and the assignment process is repeated. A final solution—which is generally achieved quite quickly—occurs when the assumed zonal characteristics upon which household assignments are based correspond to the characteristics resulting from the assignment.

CHAPTER 4

ECONOMIC AND POLICY ENVIRONMENT: 1980-1987

In this chapter we describe the assumptions and data employed to produce the Urban Institute Housing Market Simulation Model results presented in chapter 5. Data inputs fall clearly into two separate groups—those that deal with the overall economy and those that reflect specific policy changes. Assumptions about the overall economy establish basic trends for such key factors as household incomes, operating costs, and mortgage interest rates. Then specific policy changes that affect the housing sector directly are overlaid on the broad economic trends. Each group of inputs is discussed in turn in the following sections.

Broad Economic Forces

As suggested at several points in earlier chapters, over the long term the quality of a nation's housing depends critically on its overall economic performance. Indeed, the vast improvement in American housing conditions in the postwar period was largely caused by the spectacular economic growth over the two decades ending in 1970. Therefore it is logical to begin this discussion with anticipated economic performance for the 1980-1987 period.

Our choice of national economic projections was constrained by our need for detailed projections to 1987 of the distribution of incomes for the various types of households differentiated in the model. These projections were generated at the Urban Institute in the summer of 1981 using a simulation model called TRIM2. As one would expect, simulations of future income distributions must themselves be based on macroeconomic assumptions. To be consistent, our housing sector simulations must employ the same basic assumptions as these TRIM2 simulations do.

The projection of the national economy adopted for the TRIM2 simulations is the summer 1981 "cyclelong" forecast prepared by Data Resources, Inc. Clearly, a projection done so early in the simulation period may be somewhat wide of the mark. Moreover, the summer 1981 forecast omits the impact of the massive tax cuts effected by ERTA.[1] Table 12 presents a few key economic indicators for the 1981-1987 period, as projected in the summer of 1981. The figures for 1983 illustrate several points. Consumer prices in 1983 were actually much lower than projected, the unemployment rate was higher, and the federal deficit was much higher. Thus the short-term differences between the projections and reality are substantial.

It is interesting that the results of a similar forecast for 1987 done in the winter of 1982-1983 (shown in the last column of table 12) are not dramatically different for most indicators from the endpoint of the summer 1981 projection.[2] The projected paths followed by the economy to get to this point do differ sharply, but average per capita personal income levels (before taxes) and real GNP in 1987 are very close to each other under the two sets of projections. Because the Urban Institute Model uses only end-of-period income data, these income differences should have only moderate effects on the precision of the simulated results for the housing sector. On the other hand, the more recent projections reflect the higher prices and interest rates brought about by a large federal deficit. Therefore, as discussed late in the context of Reagan tax policy, we incorporate the 1982-1983 cyclelong price and interest rate projections into the Reagan I policy scenario although our distribution of household incomes is based on the 1981 projection.

Policy Changes

Four areas of policy change have immediate impacts on housing consumption or production: housing assistance policy; other aspects of income support policy; tax policy, specifically the Economic Recovery Tax Act of 1981 (ERTA); and federal policy on regulation of the thrift industry.

---

1. Only the extremely high cost of running the TRIM2 simulations under a different set of economic assumptions prevented us from doing so. The TRIM2 projections used here were developed for another purpose, and we were able to adapt them to our particular needs.
2. Projections of these values are as follows:

	1981 Projection	Winter 1981-1983 Projection
Per capita personal income	$5,121	$5,171
GNP (in billions of 1972 dollars)	1,759	1,789

Economic and Policy Environment: 1980-1987

TABLE 12

Projections of National Economic Performance, 1981-1987

	\multicolumn{7}{c}{Projections Done}
		Summer 1981					Winter 1982
Indicator	1981	1982	1983	1984	1985	1986	1987(1)	1987(2)
Consumer Price Index, percentage change (all items, all urban consumers)	10.0	8.7	7.9	7.9	10.7	9.2	7.9	9.1
Unemployment rate	7.3	6.7	6.7	6.6	6.0	6.9	7.6	7.3
Annual rate of change in GNP	2.7	3.0	3.2	4.2	3.7	−1.6	2.2	−1.1
Mortgage interest rate	14.1	14.1	13.5	13.1	14.0	14.1	12.8	13.7
Federal budget deficit, billions of dollars	52.6	46.4	50.3	44.9	19.9	91.8	93.2	94.7

For each of these areas, we present a summary of developments and then outline the explicit treatment of these changes in the simulation model. For purposes of the policy simulations, we actually needed two specifications for the model—a base case, reflecting the changes actually occurring in Reagan's first term, and a counterfactual case, based on our judgment of what would have occurred under a second Carter administration. For ease of reference, these are referred to as the Reagan I program and the Carter II program.

Housing Assistance Policy

The key to understanding changes in this area is recognizing that housing assistance has historically been a nonentitlement program that aids renter households.[3] Thus the critical statistic each year is the additional number of households eligible for assistance that actually begin receiving it. As the figures in table 13 indicate, the Reagan administration has dramatically reduced this number.

The figures in the table also reflect the second major change effected by the administration. Traditionally, the federal government aided families by providing housing units in projects whose development had been

---

3. This is not strictly true. A few hundred thousand homeowners were assisted in the early 1970s under the Section 235 program.

TABLE 13

TRENDS IN ASSISTED HOUSING PROGRAMS
ADMINISTERED BY THE DEPARTMENT OF HOUSING AND URBAN DEVELOPMENT,
1977–1984

Fiscal Year	Net Incremental Units[a] (In Thousands)	Percentage New Construction and Substantial Rehabilitation
1977	388	52
1978	326	55
1979	325	61
1980	187	63
1981	177	43
1982	52	12
1983	50	[c]
1984[b]	89	5

SOURCE: R. Struyk, N. Mayer, and J. Tuccillo, *Federal Housing Policy at Reagan's Mid-Term* (Washington, D.C.: The Urban Institute Press, 1983), tables 1 and 11.

a. Net incremental units is the gross number of incremental units to be assisted, less conversions of units from one program to another and the cancellation or deobligation of units for which funds were appropriated in prior years.

b. Estimated.

c. Percentage new construction and substantial rehabilitation is negative owing to deobligations.

subsidized. Since 1974, however, assistance has also been available to families that rent existing units in the open market. Thus each year the federal program involves support for a mix of new (and substantially rehabilitated) units and existing units. The cost to the federal government of providing assistance with a new unit has been about double that of doing so with an existing unit. Of course, leasing an existing unit does not increase the number of units in the housing stock. Because of the comparatively high cost of building new projects, the Reagan administration strongly favored emphasizing use of the existing housing stock. It has been very successful in achieving this objective, even succeeding in canceling projects for which funds had already been appropriated.

The final area of change in housing policy concerns eligibility and benefit levels. Under Reagan, eligibility has been more sharply focused by limiting new program participants almost exclusively to households with incomes that are less than 50 percent of the local median family income. Nationally this average is about 133 percent of the poverty level. Benefit levels have been cut in two ways. First, the share of income participants must contribute to their rent payments will rise from 25 percent to 30 percent. This applies to all programs. The second benefit cut affects only those in the program under which the family leases existing housing, the

Economic and Policy Environment: 1980-1987

so-called Section 8 existing program.[4] The rent level used by the government in computing benefits, the fair market rent, was initially to be lowered appreciably. Specifically, these rents have been set since 1974 at the 50th percentile of the rent distribution for units occupied in the past year by a new occupant. The Reagan administration advocated a change to the 40th percentile rent for all units.[5] In the summer of 1983, the administration, under strong pressure from Congress, established the 45th percentile for recent movers as the new standard. The original administration package would reduce the benefits to those in the Section 8 existing program on the order of 40 percent and would strongly discourage participation by some households.

Table 14 summarizes the housing assistance policies simulated as the Reagan I and Carter II programs. The Reagan I program is set at 50,000 additional units per year. This figure is somewhat smaller than that actually realized (see table 13), but it is much larger than the "no incremental units" proposed by the president in the 1983 budget submitted to Congress. The Carter II program is substantially larger than the Reagan I program. However, compared with the programs passed in fiscal years 1977-1979, it is somewhat smaller and deemphasizes new construction. These differences are in accord with our expectations of the direction in which housing assistance policy would have evolved in a second Carter adminis-

TABLE 14

Simulated Housing Assistance Policies
For The Reagan I and Carter II Programs

	Reagan I Program	*Carter II Program*
Additional assisted housing, units per year		
Total	50,000	250,000
New construction	10,000	100,000
Existing	40,000	150,000
Tenant contribution rate, as percentage of income	30	25
Fair market rents for existing housing	40th percentile, all units	50th percentile, recent movers

---

4. These changes are detailed in R. Struyk, N. Mayer, and J. Tuccillo, *Housing Policy at President Reagan's Mid-Term* (Washington, D.C.: The Urban Institute Press, 1983), chapter 6.

5. Both distributions exclude those units that do not meet certain minimum physical standards.

tration. The available units under both administrations are allocated to metropolitan areas on the basis of the "fair share formula" used until recently by the Department of Housing and Urban Development to distribute resources geographically. The original fair market rent levels proposed by the Reagan administration and approved by the Congress are used for the Reagan I program on the grounds that they in fact represent the administration's policy.

A final note on housing assistance policy concerns our treatment of federally sponsored rehabilitation, aside from that tied directly to housing assistance. During the 1970s, the federal government was involved in housing rehabilitation primarily through a below-market interest rate direct loan program (Section 312) and the Community Development Block Grant (CDBG) program. Together these programs provided subsidies of over $1 billion annually mostly to homeowners but to some owner-investors as well. The Section 312 program has been discontinued under Reagan, except for funds available from loan repayments, and the funding of the CDBG program has fallen by about one-third in constant dollars from fiscal year 1980 to fiscal year 1984. These reductions are not explicitly considered in our policy simulations. They must be neglected because they could not be isolated in the calibration of the model to the 1973–1980 period. This makes it impossible to segregate them in the policy simulations, since their effects are embodied in the supply function parameter values.[6] Thus the policy results will indicate a slightly better housing situation than would be the case if we could isolate these federal housing rehabilitation cuts and if, as seems likely, these funds would not be replaced by state and local governments.

Welfare Policy

The Reagan administration has achieved substantial changes in the set of programs designed to aid households with economic, health, and social problems. A general sense of the course of events is provided by the figures in table 15, which shows the trends in the importance of social programs in the federal budget. Moreover, table 15 distinguishes between programs available only to lower income households ("L programs") and those more widely available ("A programs"). It should be noted that the data for fiscal year 1984 and beyond are based on the administration's 1984 budget request and as such, probably overstate the total shift away from social spending. In any event, these data show an overall reduction in social programs as a share of total federal spending (columns 1 and 2) and the further shift away from means-tested programs (columns 3 and 4).

---

6. One reason for our inability to isolate these effects is the lack of information on the amount and form of rehabilitation subsidies in individual SMSAs.

TABLE 15

Trends in Federal Social Programs by
Type of Program, 1965-1988

Fiscal year	Expenditures as a Percentage of Total Federal Expenditures		Expenditures as a Percentage of Total Social Program Expenditures	
	A Programs	L Programs	A Programs	L Programs
1965	24	6	80	20
1970	29	9	77	23
1975	40	13	76	24
1980	41	13	75	25
1981	42	13	76	24
1982	42	11	79	21
1983	43	11	80	20
1984	42	10	80	20
1988	40	9	82	18

Source: J.A. Meyer, "Budget Cuts in the Reagan Administration: A Question of Fairness." Paper presented at The Urban Institute Conference on An Assessment of the Reagan Administration's Social Welfare Policies, 1983, tables 6 and 7.

Note: A programs are social programs for which all income groups are eligible; L programs are social programs for which only low-income persons are eligible.

Further information on the cuts experienced by lower income families in two of the most important means-tested programs—AFDC and Food Stamps—is presented in table 16. These figures show that the poorest families have been essentially protected from reductions in these programs, while the near-poor have experienced larger cuts on average. Furthermore, it should be recognized that the benefit reductions experienced by those actually participating at the start of the period are much larger than the average values for both participants and nonparticipants shown in the table. The tax-cut figures in table 16 are discussed in the next section.

The cuts in AFDC and Food Stamps clearly affect the amount of money that recipients have to spend on housing and therefore should be incorporated into our simulation analysis. The effects of cuts in these programs on household incomes in 1987 were simulated using the TRIM2 model mentioned earlier. Solutions of this model are the source of the figures in table 16. These solutions incorporate most of the changes made in the Omnibus Reconciliation Act of 1981 but not changes enacted since. The output of the model allows one to identify specific income changes for each household whose income is simulated. We have used this feature to develop "no-change" income distributions that only incorporate underlying macroeconomic conditions. The cuts in AFDC benefits are applied to the incomes of model households with the appropriate characteristics in the Urban Institute model.

TABLE 16

EFFECT OF 1981 CHANGES IN PERSONAL INCOME TAXES, AFDC,
AND FOOD STAMPS ON THE INCOMES OF FAMILIES
BY INCOME CLASS
(IN 1980 DOLLARS)

Income Class[a] ($)	Number of Families[b] (1,000)	Taxes ($)	AFDC ($)	Food Stamps ($)	Total ($)	Total (%)
Below 3,750	6,207	−6	−3	−2	−11	−0.5
3,750–7,500	13,803	−21	−12	−3	−36	−0.6
7,500–11,250	13,736	40	−15	−7	18	0.2
11,250–15,000	12,521	188	−9	−3	176	1.3
15,000–18,750	11,184	366	−2	−1	364	2.2
18,750–26,250	17,003	549	0	0	549	2.5
26,250–37,500	11,198	1,088	0	0	1,088	3.5
37,500–52,500	4,236	2,277	0	0	2,277	5.3
Over 52,500[c]	822	4,694	0	0	4,694	7.4
Average	90,711	460	−7	−2	451	2.7

Columns under "Changes in Family Income Owing to Changes in"

SOURCE: J. Palmer and I.V. Sawhill, *The Reagan Experiment* (Washington, D.C.: The Urban Institute Press, 1982), table 18-8.

a. Income is net after federal income taxes, FICA taxes, cash transfers, and Food Stamps.

b. The numbers include both families and unrelated individuals.

c. Earned incomes are capped at about $57,000 ($50,000 in 1979 dollars) for each individual earner in the household. Thus average income from all sources less taxes and transfers for this group is $63,758.

Because the Annual Housing Survey data base used in calibrating the model does not identify Food Stamp recipients and does not include the value of this assistance in income, we have ignored income changes from this source. Likewise, cuts in other programs, such as postponement of cost-of-living increases in Social Security and the application of tougher standards for eligibility for disability benefits, have not been incorporated. Thus the incomes used in the model probably understate income reductions caused by Reagan administration policy and give a slightly more positive picture of housing conditions than is warranted. In the Carter II program simulations it is assumed that there is no change in the AFDC program.

Tax Policy

The major development in tax policy in the Reagan administration, of course, was the passage of ERTA. Two sets of its many provisions are per-

Economic and Policy Environment: 1980-1987 43

tinent here—the reductions in marginal tax rates for the personal income tax and the changes in the treatment of income from rental properties.

The reductions in personal income tax rates are evident in the figures in column 2 ("taxes") of table 16. The massive relief to wealthier households is striking. It is important to understand that in generating these particular figures we assume that the tax burden faced by households at a given income level is constant over the 1980-1984 period after adjusting for inflation.[7] That is, these figures show the impact of the tax cut in a world free of inflation. Computed in this way, the tax rates of low-income households are essentially unchanged. This is because the provisions of the income tax that benefit the poor, the standard deduction, personal exemptions, and the earned income tax credit, were not altered. On this basis, taxes decline on average by 15 percent.

Changes in personal tax rates are handled directly in the model. As detailed in appendix A, the after-tax income of each model household is computed by the model, based on the household's tenure, household size, and before-tax income. Thus applying the new tax rates is straightforward. For the Carter II program, marginal tax rates, the standard deduction, and personal exemptions are all indexed, beginning in 1981. This treatment assumes that a second Carter administration would not have tolerated the extreme bracket creep caused by inflation and would, at a minimum, have held real tax rates at their 1980 levels. Comparative tax rates by taxable income class in 1980 and in the Carter II and Reagan I policy scenarios are shown in table 17. These figures are in nominal dollars and are not adjusted to 1980 dollars, as the figures in table 16 are.

One effect of the sizable reductions in marginal tax rates for upper income households is to reduce the value of deductions. Given the importance of property tax and mortgage interest deductions to upper income owners, the incidence of "trading up" and of purchasing larger and more commodious dwellings will be reduced. In addition, the very high interest rates of 1981 and 1982 stunted the rate of growth in the appreciation of house prices, which, in combination with permanently higher interest rates, has lowered the return on owner-occupied housing as an investment. Moreover, the attractiveness of homeownership has been reduced by the increased profitability of investment in nonresidential capital resulting from other ERTA provisions.[8] To account for these changes in the relative

---

7. The alternative basis for viewing these changes is the assumption of no change in tax rates. For a comparison of these two reference points, see J. Palmer and I.V. Sawhill, *The Reagan Experiment* (Washington, D.C.: The Urban Institute Press, 1982), pp. 475-477.

8. On this point, see P.H. Hendershott and J.D. Shilling, "Capital Allocation and the Economic Recovery Tax Act of 1981," *Public Finance Quarterly*, vol. 10, no. 2 (April 1982), pp. 242-273.

TABLE 17
Federal Personal Income Tax Rate for 1980, Carter II Program and Reagan I Program

Taxable Income ($)	1980 Tax ($)	1980 Liability (%)[a]	1980 Marginal Rate (%)	Carter II Tax ($)	Carter II Liability (%)[a]	Carter II Marginal Rate (%)	Reagan I Tax ($)	Reagan I Liability (%)[a]	Reagan I Marginal Rate (%)
1,000	140	14.0	14	140	14.0	14	110	11.0	11
5,000	774	15.5	18	760	15.2	16	574	11.5	12
15,000	2,838	18.9	24	2,471	16.5	18	2,061	13.7	16
25,000	5,721	22.9	32	4,617	18.5	24	4,023	16.1	22
40,000	11,688	29.2	43	8,662	21.7	32	8,003	20.0	33
60,000	21,514	35.9	54	15,793	26.3	43	14,992	25.0	38
85,000	35,154	41.4	59	27,024	31.8	49	25,103	29.5	42
120,000	56,504	47.1	64	45,035	37.5	54	40,366	33.6	45
175,000	92,284	52.7	68	76,045	43.5	59	66,894	38.2	49
400,000	249,104	62.3	70	223,905	56.0	70	179,186	44.8	50

a. As percentage of taxable income.

attractiveness of homeownership, we have assumed for the Reagan I simulations that there will be no increase over the 1980-1987 period in the share of households that are homeowners and that appreciation in house prices will occur at only half of the rate observed for the 1970s. These factors together should reduce the demand for newly constructed units by homeowners over the simulation period from the high levels of the 1970s.

Under the Carter II program, by contrast, we assume that monetary policy would have been less restrictive so that the rate of homeownership would have risen by 2 percentage points from 1980 to 1987, consistent with available projections.[9] We believe, however, that appreciation rates would still have been reduced over the 1980-1987 period, and therefore in the Carter II simulations and the Reagan I simulations, we assume that the appreciation rate is half the rate of the 1970s.

ERTA also had significant effects on the profitability of rental housing. The relevant changes in the tax code are summarized in table 18. These provisions increase the rate at which both new and existing properties can be depreciated by allowing investors to use a fifteen-year capital recovery period. For existing properties, the accelerated depreciation rate was increased from 125 percent of declining balance to 175 percent of declining balance; for new units, the rate was reduced slightly from 200 percent to 175 percent. Analysts have estimated that with a fifteen-year ownership period, inflation at 10 percent, and a 15 percent mortgage interest rate, the long-term reduction in rents realized through increased supply would be 35 percent.[10] This is the upper-bound value and depends on no excess profits accruing to the owners of capital.

In the Reagan I policy simulations we have reduced the price per unit of housing services faced by renters by 12 percent to reflect these effects of ERTA on rental housing investment. This value was chosen on the basis of our views about the length of time it will take investors to respond to changes and the extent to which these benefits are passed on to con-

---

9. Weicher, Yap, and Jones, for example, project a 5 percentage point rise in the homeownership rate from 1980 to 1990, largely on this basis of expected high rates of inflation overall and in the price of owner-occupied housing. (See J. Weicher, L. Yap, and M. Jones, *Metropolitan Housing Needs for the 1980s* (Washington, D.C.: The Urban Institute Press, 1982.) By contrast, Downs estimates at most only a 2 percentage point rise in the homeownership rate over the decade, based in part on his views about lower future rates of return on housing, see A. Downs, *Rental Housing in the 1980s* (Washington, D.C.: The Brookings Institution, 1983) chapter 5. Likewise, Hendershott and Shilling estimate about a 2 percentage point decline in the homeownership rate over the long run owing to ERTA (see Hendershott and Shilling, "Capital Allocation and the Economic Recovery Tax Act of 1981").

10. See W.B. Brueggeman, J.D. Fisher, and J.J. Stern, "Rental Housing and the Economic Recovery Act of 1981," *Public Finance Quarterly*, vol. 10, no. 2 (April 1982), pp. 222-241.

TABLE 18
Federal Tax Treatment of Income From Rental Residential Property: Impacts of ERTA

Conventional Properties	Property Acquired Prior to 1981	Property Acquired on or After Jan. 1, 1981
Depreciation allowances, new properties	200% declining balance Sum of years digits Straight line Component	175% declining balance[a] Straight line
Depreciation allowances, existing properties	125% declining balance Component	175% declining balance[a] Straight line
Tax life/recovery period	Facts and circumstances	15, 35, and 45 years
Amortization of construction period interest and property taxes	Phase-in schedule—10-year amortization by 1982	No change
Recapture of excess depreciation	Excess of accelerated depreciation over straight line to the extent of gain taxed as ordinary income in the year of sale	No change
Regular minimum tax	15% on tax preference item less statutory exemptions	No change

Properties rented by low-income households	Property Acquired Prior to 1981	Property Acquired on or After Jan. 1, 1981
Depreciation allowances, new properties	Same as conventional	200% declining balance[a] Straight line
Depreciation allowances, existing properties	Same as conventional	200% declining balance[a] Straight line
Tax life/recovery period	Same as conventional	15, 35, and 45 years
Amortization of construction period interest and property taxes	Phase-in schedule—beginning in 1982 leading to 10-year amortization	Repealed for all properties regardless of when acquired

Economic and Policy Environment: 1980-1987

TABLE 18—Continued

Properties rented by low-income households	Property Acquired Prior to 1981	Property Acquired on or After Jan. 1, 1981
Recapture of excess depreciation	Reduction of excess depreciation at the rate of 1% for each month a property is owned beyond 100 months	No change
Regular minimum tax	Same as conventional	No change

SOURCE: W.B. Brueggeman, J.D. Fisher, and J.J. Stern, "Rental Housing and the Economic Recovery Tax Act of 1981," *Public Finance Quarterly*, vol. 10, no. 2 (April 1982), table 1.

a. Available only if 15-year capital recovery period chosen.

sumers.[11] For the Carter II simulations, we have assumed that no changes in the tax treatment of rental housing occur.

If we implement the effects of ERTA outlined earlier without incorporating any of the accompanying changes in the macroeconomic environment, we will in effect be injecting an extra $200 billion of income into the economy. Clearly this will place the Reagan I program in an extremely favorable light. Although ERTA is projected to have little long-term effect on before-tax incomes, it is expected to increase prices and interest rates. Therefore, the ERTA program is accompanied by an increase in operating costs and interest rates consistent with the winter 1982-1983 cyclelong forecast presented in table 12. The higher prices of the post-ERTA forecast accompany a slightly reduced rate of income growth relative to the summer 1981 projection. As discussed earlier, our reliance on TRIM2 income distributions commits us to the summer 1981 projection of income growth. Therefore we calculate the rate of price growth relative to income growth from the winter 1981-1982 projection and apply the resulting ratio to the income growth rate predicted in the summer 1981 forecast. This process incorporates the relative price effects of ERTA into the Reagan I simulations. This treatment still favors the Reagan I program, since we are unable to reflect increases in state and local income taxes that may have occurred to offset federal tax cuts.

---

11. The model has no way to accommodate the effect the increased profits to developers will have on increasing the production of rental housing. Thus the amount of new construction over the period simulated may be understated. Appendix A presents a full description of the formulation of housing supply in the model. As to the timing of adjustments, for information on the temporal pattern of changes in the housing inventory using Annual Housing Survey data with a stock adjustment model, see C. Rydell, K. Neels, and C. Barnett, *Price Effects of a Housing Allowance Program* (Santa Monica: The Rand Corporation, 1982).

Housing Finance

Two major pieces of legislation, the first passed in 1980 and the second in 1982, have virtually transformed the thrift industry. The impact of these changes on the housing sector will likely be great because of the central role of thrifts in providing housing finance. To illustrate this point, in the fairly representative year of 1978, thrifts provided the funds (i.e., held the mortgage as an investment) for 42 percent of all funds going into mortgages; commercial banks, the second largest investor, accounted for only 22 percent.[12]

The first of the two laws of relevance here, the Depository Institutions Deregulation and Monetary Control Act of 1980, had its primary impact on the liability powers of thrifts. In particular, this legislation called for a phasing out of interest rate ceilings over a six-year period and gave thrifts checking account powers as well. These features, aggressively implemented, have given thrifts the power to compete with other institutions for funds. As one measure of the overall competition, from January 1977 to August 1982 deposits held by savings and loan associations whose return was linked to market rates jumped from 2 percent to 69 percent of their portfolios. These changes clearly resulted in more costly short-term funds for thrifts. It also left them strongly tied to housing in terms of the assets they could hold.

The second major piece of legislation, the Depository Institutions Act of 1982—known as the Garn-St Germain Bill—expanded asset powers in the areas of consumer loans and acquisition of corporate and municipal securities. Thus there is now the potential for much more active competition for the investment of thrifts' loanable funds.[13]

The effects of these changes on mortgage interest rates relative to interest rates on other investments are rather speculative at the moment. One school of thought is that there will be little change from past patterns. The reasoning here is that mortgage-backed securities and other secondary market instruments have been effective over the past several years in allowing investable funds to flow freely between mortgages and corporate securities. The only differences remaining between rates of return in the two sectors are due to inherent differences in the attributes of the underlying debt, such as risk and holding period.

---

12. These figures are for investments (mortgage holdings), whether the institution originated the mortgage, bought it, or participated in a group of mortgages in the secondary market.

13. This competition will be restricted to some degree by the tax provisions that give institutions that hold at least 60 percent of their assets in the form of mortgages substantial tax sheltering. The maximum deductions are provided when over 80 percent of the portfolio is held in mortgages. The cost of giving up the advantage will cause many institutions to stay above this 60 percent level for some time.

Economic and Policy Environment: 1980-1987

The principal alternative argument is that the degree of substitution between corporate instruments and mortgages is overstated in the first argument. Thus thrifts' use of their new asset powers will cause a rise in the relative interest on mortgages. An educated guess is that the increase will be on the order of 50 basis points.[14] The changes effected by the Garn-St Germain Bill are so recent that the evidence on the future pattern of relative rates of return is ambiguous. For the simulations, we assume that the 50 basis-point rise occurs. For the Carter II simulations, we assume no change in the spread. The justification for this assumption is somewhat weak, as many have argued that reform of the thrift industry was necessitated by economic conditions and would have occurred under any administration. On the other hand, the Reagan administration strongly supported the Federal Reserve's very tight monetary policies for combatting inflation, which produced the extremely high interest rates that proved so ruinous to the thrifts. Under the Carter II program, a different monetary policy—at least in degree—might have lessened the pressure for reform and delayed passage of the provisions in the Garn-St Germain Bill by a couple of years.

Summary

An overview of the "policy parameters" operable in the Reagan I and Carter II simulations was presented in chapter 1, table 3. The mere listing of these differences highlights the extensiveness of the changes from a probable status quo wrought by the Reagan administration. The anticipated impact on housing conditions of the differences between the two sets of parameters is certainly large, but it is difficult to judge in the abstract because of the countervailing effects of some provisions and the secondary impacts of them all.

---

14. For a good discussion of these recent developments, see J. Tuccillo and J.L. Goodman, Jr., *The U.S. Housing Finance System and the Reagan Program* (Washington, D.C.: The Urban Institute Press, 1983).

CHAPTER 5

HOUSING IN THE 1980s: ALTERNATIVE SCENARIOS

This chapter details the results of our simulations for the 1980–1987 period. One key feature of these results is that they embody the direct and indirect effects of the macroeconomic environment and the host of changes in public policies discussed in chapter 4. In short, they provide a comprehensive evaluation of the combined effects of these many factors. Another key feature of the results is that by simulating outcomes separately for metropolitan areas in the West and Northeast Census regions, we highlight the variation in probable outcomes under different market conditions.

In evaluating how the housing consumption of urban Americans has fared under the Reagan administration, we employed two distinct standards. The first is housing conditions in 1980. Use of this standard poses essentially the same question as candidate Reagan did in his televised debate with President Carter: Are you as well housed in 1987 as you were seven years ago? The second standard is housing conditions likely to have evolved under a Democratic administration. The policies likely to have been followed in a second Carter administration were detailed in chapter 4 and were shown to differ moderately to sharply in all four policy areas—housing assistance, welfare, tax policy, and housing finance.

In considering the 1980–1987 simulation results, we concentrate on the quantity of housing services consumed, the price of housing services in the market, and the share of income that families must devote to housing. We are interested both in how the population does on average and in the situation in 1987 for particular groups defined by their income, race, and household type (e.g., husband-wife families, other families, elderly couples, and individuals). In addition, we examine how much construction of new housing occurs and the extent to which dwelling units in the active housing stock in 1980 are withdrawn by 1987.

All the simulation results reported here have been generated for two metropolitan prototypes, one representing an average of Northeastern metropolitan areas and one representing an average of metropolitan areas in the West.[1] The characteristics of these two prototypes, which are inputs to the simulation model, differ in two respects that are particularly important for determining housing market outcomes. First, in the Western metropolitan area, the increase in population, in households, from 1980 to 1987 is more than 20 percent, while in the Northeast, it is less than 5 percent. Second, the costs of producing housing services, particularly the costs of operating inputs and maintenance, increase more slowly in the West than they do in the Northeast.

In reviewing the results, we first contrast the housing situation in 1980 with that under Reagan in 1987. Then we turn to a comparison of conditions in 1987 for the Reagan I and Carter II programs. Because the simulation model is best employed in comparisons of outcomes under different policy regimes, emphasis should be given to the Carter versus Reagan results.

American Housing in 1987

If Americans continue to behave in the 1980s as they did in the 1970s, and if the policies of the first Reagan administration are sustained, what will housing conditions in urban areas be like in 1987? The figures in tables 19 and 20 document our basic findings for the Northeast and West metropolitan areas, respectively. The principal findings are that there is widespread improvement in housing consumption over the period, continuing the strong postwar trend. Higher income households experience the greatest improvement, and those at the bottom of the income distribution experience the least improvement. The results also show a broad pattern of reductions in the ratio of housing expenditures to income. Homeowners realize the largest reductions; among renters, those in the Northeast actually experience an increase, and those in the West enjoy a decline. Finally, while 22 percent of the 1980 housing stock is withdrawn over the period in the Northeast, no units are withdrawn in the West. The balance of this section reviews the events behind the results and the findings themselves in greater detail. Tables 19 and 20 present five indicators of the simulated impacts of Reagan administration policies on housing consumption and housing expenditures: permanent income, housing consumption, housing expenditures, federal taxes, and housing expense to income ratio.

---

1. A description of these prototypes is provided in appendix B.

TABLE 19
NORTHEAST: CHANGES FROM 1980 TO 1987 UNDER THE REAGAN I PROGRAM

	Permanent Income[a]	Housing Consumption[b]	Housing Expenditures[c]	Federal Taxes[d]	Housing Expense to Income Ratio[e] 1973–1980	Housing Expense to Income Ratio[e] 1980–1987
All households	79.7	50.0	62.7	91.8	0.216	0.199
Household types						
White, elderly	119.2	49.4	63.6	247.6	0.321	0.260
White, nonelderly husband-wife	73.4	49.1	62.0	84.1	0.185	0.173
White, nonelderly other	82.9	42.1	55.4	92.5	0.265	0.240
Black	100.4	70.8	75.2	137.5	0.254	0.228
Income quintiles						
1—low	91.3	38.1	42.6	411.1	0.410	0.340
2	79.3	49.3	54.9	112.9	0.270	0.241
3	74.3	44.6	62.1	81.3	0.221	0.212
4	66.4	57.7	74.6	63.5	0.192	0.189
5—high	83.2	51.6	66.1	94.3	0.173	0.159
Tenure groups						
Renters	69.7	49.1	54.7	71.1	0.236	0.252
Owners	85.8	47.6	63.5	100.8	0.201	0.180

a. Permanent income is before-tax household income, adjusted to reflect central tendencies for each household type. Table presents percentage increases from 1980 to 1987.
b. Housing consumption is the level of housing services, including structural attributes, housing quality, amenities, and operating inputs. Table presents percentage increases from 1980 to 1987.
c. Housing expenditures are out-of-pocket costs, including utilities, interest, property taxes, and maintenance. Expenditures are calculated as the product of average prices for the 1973–1980 and 1980–1987 periods and end-of-period consumption levels. Table presents percentage increases from 1980 to 1987.
d. Federal taxes are the federal income tax liability. Table presents percentage increases from 1980 to 1987.
e. Housing expense to income ratio is the ratio of housing expenditures to permanent income, both defined above. Table presents both 1980 and 1987 values for comparison.

TABLE 20

WEST: CHANGES FROM 1980 TO 1987 UNDER THE REAGAN I PROGRAM

	Permanent Income[a]	Housing Consumption[b]	Housing Expenditures[c]	Federal Taxes[d]	Housing Expense to Income Ratio[e] 1973–1980	Housing Expense to Income Ratio[e] 1980–1987
All households	76.0	66.7	39.0	86.0	0.225	0.183
Household types						
White, elderly	99.3	19.5	29.9	180.8	0.273	0.216
White, nonelderly husband-wife	68.0	62.3	33.7	75.0	0.201	0.160
White, nonelderly other	78.0	83.5	42.9	85.5	0.265	0.227
Black	91.6	73.8	57.4	139.3	0.283	0.235
Income quintiles						
1—low	79.3	54.7	32.7	200.0	0.374	0.314
2	87.2	58.0	35.5	114.3	0.265	0.213
3	71.8	67.2	43.4	76.0	0.227	0.196
4	63.5	76.8	36.4	63.6	0.206	0.169
5—high	76.3	67.8	45.5	84.8	0.188	0.145
Tenure groups						
Renters	76.8	93.8	55.0	92.2	0.261	0.253
Owners	75.2	48.1	28.2	83.5	0.211	0.158

a. Permanent income is before-tax household income, adjusted to reflect central tendencies for each household type. Table presents percentage increases from 1980 to 1987.
b. Housing consumption is the level of housing services, including structural attributes, housing quality, amenities, and operating inputs. Table presents percentage increases from 1980 to 1987.
c. Housing expenditures are out-of-pocket costs, including utilities, interest, property taxes, and maintenance. Expenditures are calculated as the product of average prices for the 1973–1980 and 1980–1987 periods and end-of-period consumption levels. Table presents percentage increases from 1980 to 1987.
d. Federal taxes are the federal income tax liability. Table presents percentage increases from 1980 to 1987.
e. Housing expense to income ratio is the ratio of housing expenditures to permanent income, both defined above. Table presents both 1980 and 1987 values for comparison.

Permanent Income

Permanent income reflects a household's current income adjusted for the longer term income expectations upon which households base major consumption decisions. Most households with low current incomes, for example, are expected to have higher permanent incomes when they end a current period of unemployment. The first column of tables 19 and 20 compares 1987 permanent incomes with 1980 permanent incomes. On average, permanent incomes (in nominal dollars) are projected to increase by about 80 percent in the Northeast and by about 75 percent in the West. In both regions, it is assumed that white, elderly households and black households, whose incomes were lowest in 1980, will experience the greatest income gains. The largest and most affluent group, white, nonelderly husband-wife households, experience slightly below-average increases. When households are disaggregated by income quintile, the poorest households in both the Northeast and West (quintiles 1 and 2) experience greater proportionate increases than do households in the third and fourth quintiles. Highest income households also do well.

Housing Consumption

Housing consumption refers to the level of housing services, including structural attributes, housing quality, amenities, and operating inputs. Under the Reagan I policies, households in the Northeast consume about 50 percent more housing services in 1987 than they did in 1980, while in the West, housing consumption increases by about 66 percent (column 2 of tables 19 and 20). From 1973 to 1980, housing consumption increased by about 47 percent in the Northeast and by about 60 percent in the West. Thus, on average, households make about the same gains in the quantity of housing services during the 1980-1987 period as they did during the 1970s.

How do households manage to achieve such substantial gains in housing consumption? Experience to date indicates that real income gains have been minimal and suggests that large increases in consumption levels may not be feasible. The Urban Institute Model results, however, show the market price of housing services growing considerably more slowly than household incomes, so that most households are able to improve their housing circumstances markedly over the 1980-1987 period. In part, this somewhat counterintuitive result stems from the model's limited capacity to differentiate price changes over a simulation period from quantity changes. Because of this limitation, we tend to have greater confidence in the comparative housing consumption outcomes of the model's Reagan I and Carter II simulations than in the 1980-1987 consumption changes.

The reasons for the slow growth in housing service prices predicted by the model differ for the Northeast and the West. In the Northeast where the housing market is relatively loose, middle- and upper-income households choose large, inexpensive existing dwellings rather than smaller, more costly new dwellings. This allows them to enjoy large housing consumption increases without incurring substantially higher prices. Moreover, the market is sufficiently loose that the demand for existing units by middle- and upper-income households does not generate excessive competition for existing units of lower quality.

In the West, on the other hand, the housing market is very tight, both in the 1970s and in the 1980s. ERTA's increased incentives for rental housing investment, however, are sufficient to attract a large number of middle- and high-income renters to new dwellings. This relieves some of the pressure on the existing housing stock and seems to prevent prices from escalating too precipitously in the market as a whole.

In both regions, the model results show housing consumption increasing dramatically for black households, partly as a result of their large projected income increases. It is interesting that white, elderly households, who enjoy above-average income increases, experience average (Northeast) or below-average (West) increases in housing consumption. This is probably due, in part, to the dramatic increase in federal income taxes paid by this group.

Changes in consumption by income quintile suggest that, generally, richer households enjoy the greatest gains. In the Northeast, the greatest increases are experienced by the two richest quintiles, and the smallest increases are experienced by the poorest quintile. In the West, the greatest increases are enjoyed by the richest three quintiles, and the two lowest quintiles fare poorly. Note, however, that the overall pattern of increases in the West is much higher than that in the Northeast: the level of housing consumption in the highest and lowest income quintiles in the two regions, respectively, are 68 and 55, and 52 and 38 units of service per month.

There are two basic reasons why high-income households are able to enjoy above-average consumption gains even though their incomes sometimes increase less dramatically than the incomes of poorer households. First, the supply of housing services from the existing stock is more price responsive in high-quality dwellings than it is in low-quality dwellings. In other words, a relatively affluent household living in a dwelling that offers a high level of services can increase the level of services significantly by bidding up the market price only slightly. Lower-income households living in poor-quality units have to increase the market price more substantially to obtain a comparable increase in the level of services. In addition, high-income households, who are predominantly homeowners, pay an after-tax housing service price that is sharply below the market price because they can deduct mortgage interest and property tax payments. Thus the *after-tax* cost of increased housing consumption is small for high-income households living in high-quality dwellings.

Simulated patterns of consumption for owners and renters differ in the two regions. In the Northeast, there is a modest difference in the proportionate increases predicted for the two tenure groups, favoring homeowners. In the West, by contrast, renters increase their consumption dramatically, and the increase for owner-occupants is below average. This somewhat surprising result seems to be explained by the fact that, in the West, where competition for the existing stock is intense, ERTA's increased tax subsidy for rental housing combined with high rental prices enables a sizable number of moderate-income renters to afford small new apartments, thereby improving their housing situation markedly.

Housing Expenditures

Housing expenditures (column 3 of tables 19 and 20) include all out-of-pocket costs: utilities, interest, property taxes, and maintenance.[2] Expenditures are calculated on the basis of average prices for the period under analysis, 1973-1980 and 1980-1987, and end-of-period consumption levels. For the most part, increases in expenditures follow increases in consumption fairly closely. However, high-income households, which enjoy greater-than-average increases in consumption, experience below-average increases in expenditures. This is particularly true in the West, where the second richest income quintile makes the greatest gain in housing consumption (77 percent) and experiences a small increase in expenditures (36 percent). As mentioned earlier, the Urban Institute model assumes that the price responsiveness of supply is greatest in high-quality dwellings, thereby allowing affluent households to enjoy large consumption gains and relatively modest increases in expenditures.[3]

Federal Taxes

Federal taxes powerfully affect housing outcomes by partially determining disposable income and the net housing price consumers face. Income taxes are approximated on the basis of personal income tax schedules using end-of-period permanent incomes. On average, estimated taxes rise by about 90 percent from 1980 to 1987, and the greatest increases are experienced by white, elderly households, black households, and the poorest income quintile. To some degree, the pattern of tax increases for these groups corresponds to the pattern of income growth, but taxes generally

---

2. Thus these are expenditures *before* tax deductions.
3. This is explained in greater detail in appendix A.

increase at least half again as much as income. This result can probably be explained by the fact that the value of tax exemptions and the standard deduction, which is overwhelmingly relied upon by low-income households, are not changed by ERTA, while income growth moves these households into higher tax brackets.

Housing Expense to Income Ratios

Housing expense to income ratios express average monthly housing expenditures for the 1973-1980 and 1980-1987 periods as a proportion of monthly permanent incomes (before taxes) in 1980 and 1987, respectively.[4] In both the Northeast and the West, the model predicts that households will spend a smaller proportion of their before-tax incomes on housing in 1987 than they did in 1980. One reason for this result is that taxes increase faster than incomes, making the ratio of disposable income to total permanent income smaller. Because disposable incomes are smaller, relative to permanent incomes, households spend somewhat less on housing, as well as on other goods and services. This argument is supported by the fact that in the Northeast, the groups with the largest drop in housing expense to income ratios, white, elderly households and the poorest income quintile, also experience the greatest increases in taxes relative to income growth. In the simulations for the West, on the other hand, all household groups and income quintiles experience roughly the same reduction in housing expense to income ratios.

Tenure differences in the West indicate that renters will spend slightly less of their income on housing in 1987 than they did in 1980, while owners will spend much less. In the Northeast, renters' expenditure ratio rises, while that for owners declines. The reason for the divergence between the results for renters in the Northeast and the results for renters in the West is that in 1980, housing prices for renters were high in the West and low in the Northeast. Over the 1980-1987 period, they remained high in the West but had to increase substantially in the Northeast so that rental properties could be profitable and continue to operate. Moreover, incomes of renters rose less in the Northeast than they did in the West.

The Reagan I Program versus the Carter II Program

Would urban America have been better housed in 1987 if Jimmy Carter had returned to the White House and implemented the policies out-

---

4. Note that these ratios differ in important ways from those typically cited. Expenditures are the product of average over-the-period prices and end-of-period quantity consumed, while the income concept is permanent, not current.

Housing in the 1980's: Alternative Scenarios

lined in chapter 4? Unfortunately, there is no simple answer. Americans' views on this question will reflect where they live and who they are. Our results are quite sensitive to the housing market conditions in 1980 and developments over the 1980-1987 period. Households in the Northeast are slightly less well housed under the stylized program attributed to Reagan than they are under that attributed to Carter, and the poor, blacks, and elderly whites are the most adversely affected. In the metropolitan areas of the West, on the other hand, housing is a little better under the Reagan policies, and real improvements are experienced by the same groups that do poorly in the Northeast.

It is important to bear in mind that the Reagan-Carter comparisons involve contrasting whole families of policies in two widely differing market environments. Consequently, the comparisons are not simple, although we have tried to present a clear summary.

Metropolitan Areas of the Northeast

The dominant difference between the two policy programs in the Northeast is the shift of households from newly built to existing housing. Before presenting these results, however, we should provide some orientation to them. The basic figures are presented in table 21. The upper panel of the table presents the differences in outcomes for the two programs on a percentage basis (Reagan minus Carter), and the lower panel gives the 1987 Carter outcomes. The first thing to note is that three groups of households experience above-average reductions in housing consumption under the Reagan I program in comparison with the Carter II program—elderly whites, blacks, and those in the lowest income groups. The changes for the other groups are negligible. Reductions in housing expenditures for these three groups are even greater, mirroring the fact that the price of housing services faced by these households is lower under the Reagan I program than it is under the Carter II program. Greater consumption at higher prices means that the ratio of housing expenditures to permanent income is higher under the Carter II program than it is under the Reagan I program for these same groups. Again, differences for other groups are negligible.

What produces these differences? The principal factor is the higher interest rates present in the Reagan I program in comparison with the Carter II program, which result primarily from the huge budget deficits but also from deregulation of the thrift industry. The effects on new construction of the interest rate differential are impressive. The level of new building (in terms of dwelling units) is about 50 percent greater in the Carter II program than it is in the Reagan I program. With the number of incremental households fixed, this increase in new units is matched by an

TABLE 21

NORTHEAST: REAGAN I VERSUS CARTER II PROGRAM OUTCOMES, 1980–1987

	Housing Service Price[a]	Housing Consumption[b]	Housing Expenditures[c]	Federal Taxes[d]	Housing Expense to Income Ratio[e] Carter II	Reagan I
All households	−3.3	−2.1	−4.3	−16.2	0.205	0.199
Household types						
White, elderly	−11.5	−3.9	−12.7	−21.1	0.301	0.260
White, nonelderly husband-wife	−0.4	−0.9	−0.9	−17.7	0.170	0.173
White, nonelderly other	−3.1	−1.7	−4.6	−10.1	0.251	0.240
Black	−3.2	−5.3	−8.4	−17.7	0.249	0.228
Income quintiles						
1—low	−7.8	−9.0	−16.3	−9.8	0.405	0.340
2	−7.4	−2.2	−9.8	−14.9	0.265	0.241
3	−2.6	0.8	−2.1	−14.1	0.217	0.212
4	0.3	0.0	0.2	−18.5	0.186	0.189
5—high	0.7	−0.5	0.4	−15.1	0.156	0.159
Tenure groups						
Renters	−7.2	0.8	−6.0	−1.9	0.282	0.252
Owners	0.3	−2.2	−2.1	−15.8	0.183	0.180

Housing in the 1980's: Alternative Scenarios

Base Case, Carter II Program (1987)

	Housing Service Price[a]	Housing Consumption[b]	Housing Expenditures[c]	Federal Taxes[d]
All households	1.974	285	556	419
Household types				
White, elderly	2.037	255	516	185
White, nonelderly husband-wife	2.012	319	633	662
White, nonelderly, other	2.014	237	479	227
Black	1.614	303	486	231
Income quintiles				
1—low	1.905	211	400	51
2	2.001	229	457	175
3	2.019	254	512	304
4	2.023	306	617	534
5—high	1.918	416	781	998
Tenure groups				
Renters	1.904	238	451	157
Owners	2.017	314	623	584

NOTE: The top panel of the table presents percentage differences between Reagan I and Carter II program outcomes, with Carter II results as the base. The bottom panel presents the Carter II program results.

a. Housing service price is the average market price per unit (per month) of housing services for the 1980–1987 period.
b. Housing consumption is the 1987 level of housing services (per month), including structural attributes, housing quality, amenities, and operating inputs.
c. Housing expenditures are monthly out-of-pocket costs, including interest, utilities, property taxes, and maintenance, calculated from the average 1980–1987 price of housing services and the 1980 consumption level.
d. Federal taxes are monthly taxes, calculated from personal income tax schedules on the basis of 1987 permanent income.
e. Housing expense to income ratio is the ratio of average 1980–1987 housing expenditures to 1987 before-tax permanent income.

equal number of units withdrawn from the active housing stock. Thus the market is quite loose and is characterized by low prices per unit of services among those dwellings providing the lowest levels of services. On the other hand, new units all have the same (higher) price per unit of service, which is competitive with the price commanded by high-quality existing dwellings. This means that the occupants of the new units—who are primarily moderate-income households and 60 percent of whom are homeowners—pay this relatively high price under the Carter II program.

The higher interest rates of the Reagan I program make the new construction alternative less attractive to the moderate-income households. A number of those who occupy new units in the Carter II program are in existing units in the Reagan I program. Note that these existing units command a price per unit of service that is lower than that for new units. Moreover, because the level of new construction falls sharply, the overall observed price per unit of service in 1987 is lower under the Reagan I program than it is under the Carter II program. Under Reagan I two-thirds of the occupants of new units are in the highest two income quintiles and are exclusively nonelderly whites. They are split 40–60 between owners and renters, as they are under the Carter II program.

To summarize, greater housing consumption and higher prices of housing services under the Carter II program are concentrated among the elderly, blacks, and the lowest income households. This is largely attributable to the higher interest rates under the Reagan I program, which sharply reduce the amount of new construction occurring. On balance, some households shift from higher priced, smaller new units under the Carter II program to lower priced, larger existing units under the Reagan I program. Also note that more existing dwellings are retained in the active stock under the Reagan I program—a significant benefit to struggling central cities.

Metropolitan Areas in the West

The urban housing markets in the West in the 1980s are tight markets getting tighter. The contrast between the West and Northeast in housing situations in 1980, reviewed in chapter 2, was stark; the results for Reagan I versus Carter II programs in the 1980s are in even higher relief. The summary information in table 22 shows that in the West, overall consumption is higher under the Reagan I program (in the Northeast it is lower). Three of the groups whose consumption increase is greater than the average under the Reagan I program are the white elderly, blacks, and the poorest households; these same groups in the Northeast do least well under the Reagan I program in comparison with the Carter II program. Overall the price per unit of housing services in the West is lower under the Reagan I program than it is under the Carter II program (as it is the Northeast). But the lower prices do not offset the increase in consumption, so that the ratio of housing expense to permanent income is greater for the Reagan I policy package than it is for the Carter II package. Black households, white, nonelderly husband-wife households, and middle-income households generally experience higher ratios under the Reagan I program.

The explanation for these outcomes again has to do with the differences in the pattern of new construction, but the results diverge sharply from those for the Northeast. A key difference between the Northeast and the West in the 1980s is that while under both the Carter II and Reagan I programs there is substantial surplus housing in the Northeast, *no* units are withdrawn in the West under either policy program. This tightness, however, does not prevent broad-based improvement in housing conditions.

Under the Carter II program, the lower interest rates are not sufficient to induce a large number of middle- and higher-income households to select new units, as they are able to find existing units suitable to their needs. Consequently, competition in the lower half of the market is extremely intense. New construction is concentrated among small rental units. Even so, 3 percent of all households, and 15 percent of the poorest, are forced to double up, which substantially increases the price of services to these households.[5]

The Reagan I program produces a different pattern of new construction. In particular, the increase in disposable incomes resulting from the ERTA tax cuts encourages middle- and higher-income households to occupy new units, even though the price per unit of services from new units is somewhat higher under the Reagan I program than it is under the Carter II program. This produces about 16 percent more new construction, which is sufficient to relieve the crowding experienced under the Carter II program. Still, most of the new construction is of rental units, reflecting the provisions of ERTA favorable to apartment development and the effects of reduced appreciation on the net price of owner-occupied housing. This pattern of new construction cools the white-hot competition among the lowest income households and produces the favorable pattern of prices for these households observed under the Reagan I program. Households that

---

5. In the Urban Institute Model, discrete model households, each representing several hundred actual households, are allocated across discrete model dwellings, each representing a comparable number of actual dwellings. Each model household must select one model dwelling; there is no mechanism within the model to allow households to "double up." Therefore, in situations in which crowding is likely to occur, the model solution simply yields one or more model households that have not been allocated to model dwellings. When this occurs, we assume that the unallocated households are doubling up with households that occupy the poorest dwellings in the existing stock. It is assumed that two model households that share a model dwelling split the equilibrium quantity of housing services and pay 130 percent of the equilibrium price. Model results are then adjusted to reflect these circumstances.

TABLE 22
WEST: REAGAN I VERSUS CARTER II PROGRAM OUTCOMES, 1980–1987

	Housing Service Price[a]	Housing Consumption[b]	Housing Expenditures[c]	Federal Taxes[d]	Housing Expense to Income Ratio[e] Carter II	Reagan I
All households	−2.4	4.4	3.8	−14.7	0.177	0.183
Household types						
White, elderly	−3.5	12.6	6.7	−19.3	0.216	0.216
White, nonelderly husband-wife	1.8	2.1	4.6	−15.1	0.151	0.160
White, nonelderly other	−4.8	10.7	2.3	−8.2	0.226	0.227
Black	−6.4	−7.0	−0.7	−23.9	0.219	0.235
Income quintiles						
1—low	−13.6	16.8	4.1	−10.4	0.320	0.314
2	−1.4	3.9	1.9	−13.3	0.209	0.213
3	−0.8	6.1	4.3	−14.2	0.187	0.196
4	2.1	4.9	6.3	−16.1	0.157	0.169
5—high	3.7	0.0	3.2	−13.5	0.139	0.145
Tenure groups						
Renters	−8.7	11.0	2.4	−5.7	0.257	0.253
Owners	1.9	0.7	4.9	−14.4	0.151	0.158

Housing in the 1980's: Alternative Scenarios

BASE CASE, CARTER II PROGRAM (1987)

	Housing Service Price[a]	Housing Consumption[b]	Housing Expenditures[c]	Federal Taxes[d]
All households	1.775	297	505	469
Household types				
White, elderly	2.092	174	342	181
White, nonelderly husband-wife	1.714	337	565	676
White, nonelderly other	1.768	281	479	279
Black	1.700	273	455	264
Income quintiles				
1—low	1.916	184	343	77
2	1.843	228	416	225
3	1.770	279	488	359
4	1.713	327	553	589
5—high	1.589	458	719	1069
Tenure groups				
Renters	1.710	281	468	210
Owners	1.812	306	529	624

NOTE: The top panel of the table presents percentage differences between Reagan I and Carter II program outcomes, with Carter II results as the base. The bottom panel presents the Carter II program results.

a. Housing service price is the average market price per unit (per month) of housing services for the 1980–1987 period.
b. Housing consumption is the 1987 level of housing services (per month), including structural attributes, housing quality, amenities, and operating inputs.
c. Housing expenditures are monthly out-of-pocket costs, including interest, utilities, property taxes, and maintenance, calculated from the average 1980–1987 price of housing services and the 1980 consumption level.
d. Federal taxes are monthly taxes, calculated from personal income tax schedules on the basis of 1987 permanent income.
e. Housing expense to income ratio is the ratio of average 1980–1987 housing expenditures to 1987 before-tax permanent income.

were forced to double up under the Carter II program end up in larger units with a lower price per unit of housing services under the Reagan I program. At the same time, however, the generally higher prices for inputs, including capital, present under the Reagan I program mean higher housing prices for homeowners and virtually no change in consumption. This leads to higher housing expense to permanent income ratios under the Reagan I program, in comparison with the Carter II program.

In the West, then, the cut in income taxes and tax breaks for rental property developers by the Reagan administration are key to fueling the demand for new rental housing by middle-income families. This stimulates more building than that experienced under the Carter II policies and relieves the intense competition for housing among lower income households. This is a case in which the filtering strategy clearly works.

Concluding Observations

The good news is that the quality of housing occupied by Americans living in urban areas would have improved substantially over the 1980-1987 period, regardless of whether Reagan I or Carter II policies were in effect. On the basis of the results developed here it is impossible to say that one program would have been unequivocally better, either for all households on average or for important subgroups of the population. One reason for the ambiguity is the offsetting effects of the policies included in both the Reagan I and Carter II packages, which create a kind of stalemate. But the central reason for this result is the sensitivity of outcomes under a given set of policies to conditions in the urban housing market in which the policies are implemented. Several aspects of the market environment clearly influenced the results reviewed earlier. The distribution of disposable income, and thus the income tax structure, is important, as are the tax incentives for developing new rental housing and the rate of appreciation on housing investments. Perhaps most pervasive, however, are differences in the rate at which markets are growing in terms of the number of households. A final key relationship is that between the initial housing stock, and its ability to be altered, and the changing preferences of households for housing, which are driven by income growth and shifts in the age, race, and composition of households.

Also evident in these results is the substantial degree of segmentation present in urban housing markets. This is clearest in the patterns of new construction in which production is concentrated for certain income and tenure groups. More generally, pressures in one part of the market are not always easily relieved because of the limits to which dwellings existing at the start of the period can be modified to suit the new demand structure. Thus we have observed uneven patterns of prices, crowding, and consumption changes across income groups.

The foregoing observations lead to a final comment. With market outcomes influenced by so many different factors, it is expected that imposing complex sets of policies on them would produce results that are both difficult to anticipate and highly variable with differences in the market environment.

Moreover, the results presented in this chapter indicate the overwhelming power of local market trends in the number of households, disposable income, and housing prices in determining how well the poor, as well as the rich, are housed and in determining the ultimate impact of national policy initiatives.

In this context, matching the use of housing assistance resources to local market conditions is essential. In fact, such matching was the thrust of the Housing and Community Development Act of 1974. The Housing Assistance Plan, formally part of a city's application for CDBG funds, was an important step in properly deploying available housing funds.[6] Unfortunately, the ability of local governments to design their own plans has been reduced by the Reagan administration's proposals—approved by Congress—that almost eliminated construction of new projects and substantial rehabilitation of others to aid the poor. While this can be justified in most markets on the basis of the lower cost of renting existing units in comparison with building new ones, in very tight markets some relief at the lower end is probably essential.[7] Moreover, the reduction in emphasis on formulation of a local plan seems especially short-sighted.

---

6. For more on the early history of Housing Assistance Plans in metropolitan areas, see R. Struyk and J. Khadduri, "Saving the Housing Assistance Plan: Improving Incentives to Local Governments," *American Planning Association Journal* vol. 4, no. 4 (October 1980), pp. 387–397.

7. An extended discussion of this point is presented in M. Isler, "Policy Implications: Moving from Research to Programs," in R. Struyk and M. Bendick, Jr., eds., *Housing Vouchers for the Poor* (Washington, D.C.: The Urban Institute Press, 1981).

APPENDIX A

THE URBAN INSTITUTE HOUSING MARKET SIMULATION MODEL: THEORY AND SOLUTION PROCESS

The Urban Institute Housing Market Simulation Model is a tool for analyzing long-term (seven- to ten-year) changes in housing quality, housing expenditures, and household location within metropolitan areas. The changes analyzed are caused by shifts in such factors as household incomes, the rate of population growth, alterations in government housing policies aimed at assisting the poor, and monetary policy effects on interest rates.

The Urban Institute Model is a mature modeling effort; initial model development occurred in the early 1970s.[1] Since the first development effort, the model has undergone significant changes. A version for use in the context of developing countries was formulated.[2] Perhaps most significant, MacRae developed a dramatically more efficient solution algorithm for the model.[3] From the start the Urban Institute Model was developed to analyze the impacts and efficiency of public interventions in the housing sector, with particular emphasis on the differential effects of the same interventions across metropolitan areas with different housing stock, population growth, and income distribution characteristics.[4]

---

1. See F. de Leeuw and R. Struyk, *The Web of Urban Housing: Analyzing Policy with a Market Simulation Model* (Washington, D.C.: The Urban Institute Press, 1975).
2. See, for example, R. Struyk, "A Simulation Model of Urban Housing Markets in Developing Countries," Working Paper 5062-1 (Washington, D.C.: The Urban Institute, 1976).
3. See C.D. MacRae, "Urban Housing with Discrete Structures," *Journal of Urban Economics*, vol. 11 (1982), pp. 131-147.
4. See, for example, R. Struyk, S.A. Marshall, and L. Ozanne, *Housing Policies for the Urban Poor* (Washington, D.C.: The Urban Institute Press, 1978); J. Vanski and L. Ozanne, *Simulating the Housing Allowance Program in Green Bay and South Bend* (Washington, D.C.: The Urban Institute Press, 1978); and M. Andreassi and C.D. MacRae, *Homeowner*

This appendix describes in detail the structure of the conceptual framework and solution process of the model resulting from the most recent developmental effort. The discussion consists of two sections: theoretical framework and solution process. The division in subject matter is less strict than these labels indicate, as we have found it expositionally more lucid to present some details of theory in the discussion of the solution process. Elaboration of the reasons for particular assumptions made in the formulation are provided elsewhere.[5]

Theoretical Framework

In the Urban Institute Model, a metropolitan housing market is represented by several dozen "model" households, several dozen "model" dwellings, and a new construction industry. Each model household represents several hundred or thousand actual households, and each model dwelling represents a comparable number of actual dwellings. The metropolitan area is divided into a small number of zones, each with accessibility, wealth, and racial attributes. The model simulates the behavior of individual owner-occupant and renter households seeking a place to live, of dwelling owners offering housing services at various prices, and of a building industry meeting demands for new construction at an acceptable rate of return.

The current version of the model incorporates the effects of federal income tax provisions that allow owner-occupant households to deduct their mortgage interest and property tax payments as well as provisions that allow landlords to benefit from accelerated depreciation deductions. These provisions can alter both the effective price of housing services and a household's disposable income, thereby influencing the quantity of housing services consumed. Inclusion of federal tax provisions complicates the Urban Institute Model's original theoretical framework considerably. In effect, the model now encompasses three housing service demand func-

---

Income Tax Provisions and Metropolitan Housing Markets (Washington, D.C.: The Urban Institute Press, 1981). The model has been subjected to a number of reviews over the years. See R. Mohan, *Urban Economic and Planning Models: Assessing the Potential for Cities in Developing Countries* (Baltimore, Md.: The Johns Hopkins University Press, 1979); B. Hamilton, "Discussion," in R.H. Haveman and K. Hollbeck, eds., *Microeconomic Simulation Models for Public Policy Analysis: Vol. 2* (New York: Academic Press, 1980), pp. 204-207; and E.O. Olsen, "Discussion," in R.H. Haveman and K. Hollbeck, eds., *Microeconomic Simulation Models for Public Policy Analysis: Vol. 2* (New York: Academic Press, 1980), pp. 208-212.

5. See de Leeuw and Struyk, *The Web of Urban Housing*; Struyk, "A Simulation Model of Urban Housing Markets in Developing Countries"; and MacRae, "Urban Housing with Discrete Structures."

tions: one for renters, one for owners who claim the standard deduction, and one for owners who itemize their deductions. The model also includes two supply functions: one for the owners of existing dwellings and one for the construction of new units.

The remainder of this section presents theoretical rules that govern the behavior of dwelling owners, the new construction industry, and households.

Existing Dwelling Supply

Housing services are supplied by the owners of model dwellings built over the simulation period and by the owners of existing model dwellings. When an existing dwelling is occupied by a renter household, the producer of housing services is the landlord. Owner-occupant households effectively act as their own landlords. It is assumed that landlords and owner-occupant households face the same production costs and maximize profits subject to the same production function. Therefore, the supply function governing the production of housing services from a model dwelling does not vary with the tenure of the model household that occupies that dwelling.

The assumption of a single production function, applicable to both landlords and owner-occupants, may seem inappropriate given differences in federal income tax benefits. However, we treat both the accelerated depreciation deductions available for rental housing and the mortgage interest and property tax deductions available for owner-occupied housing as reductions in the effective price of services perceived by the consumer, not as reductions in the supply costs perceived by the producer.

In other words, we assume that tax benefits are entirely passed on to housing service consumers. This assumption is entirely reasonable for owner-occupants, who behave simultaneously as producers and consumers, but somewhat less obvious for renters. However, if landlords retain the special tax benefits available for housing, their profits will exceed normal levels. Ultimately, new investment will be attracted to rental housing by the opportunity to earn profits, and landlords will be forced to reduce their rents to attract tenants. Thus in the long term, one would expect tax benefits to be largely passed on to housing service consumers in the form of lower rents.[6] The magnitude of the tax benefits enjoyed by housing service consumers is discussed separately for owners and renters in the section on household demand.

Housing services are supplied by the owners of existing dwellings according to a production function that expresses the current level of housing

---

6. See F. de Leeuw and L. Ozanne, "The Impact of Federal Income Tax on Investment in Housing," *Survey of Current Business*, vol. 59, no. 12 (December 1979), pp. 50-61.

services (Q) in terms of an initial level of services (Q_o) and a quantity of newly added capital inputs (K^*),

$$Q = [\beta_1 + (2\beta_2 K^*/Q_o)^{.5}]Q_o.$$

This production function implies that, if an owner fails to add any new capital inputs to an existing dwelling, the level of services produced will depreciate at a rate of $1 - \beta_1$. New capital inputs must be added to maintain or increase the level of services. The effectiveness of capital additions depends both on the quantity of housing services provided by a unit at the start of the period being simulated (Q_o) and on the amount of new capital added (K^*). The level of housing services can be augmented most readily in dwellings with relatively large values of Q_o, and in all dwellings, the marginal productivity of new capital inputs declines as K^* increases.

Profits earned by the owners of existing dwellings (π) consist of rent revenues (PQ) less operating expenditures (oQ) and capital costs. Capital costs include interest (ρ), property taxes (τ), and real depreciation (μ), both on capital embodied in the unit at the beginning of the period (K_o) and on new capital inputs added during the current period (K^*).[7] Thus producer profits can be expressed as

$$\pi = PQ - oQ - (\rho + \tau + \mu)(K_o + K^*).$$

Note that capital costs are assumed to be the same for both new and existing capital inputs. This assumption is reasonable when we consider that, over the course of a decade, most existing dwelling owners sell or refinance, bringing their capital costs up to new dwelling levels. Moreover, owners who do not sell or refinance accrue a substantial amount of equity during a decade, and the opportunity cost on their equity can reasonably be approximated by the new capital inputs price.

Maximizing profit subject to the housing service production function yields a supply function of

$$Q = [\beta_1 + \beta_2 (P - o)/(\rho + \tau + \mu)]Q_o.$$

This function is only valid when the price of housing services (P) realized by a dwelling owner equals or exceeds the price of operating inputs (o). For lower values of P, a model dwelling is assumed to be withdrawn from the market; no dwellings will be occupied by households that pay a unit price less than o. When P is equal to o, the supply function implies that no new

---

7. Note that Q is a direct function of K, via the production function for the previous period.

Appendix A

capital inputs are added, and the quantity of housing services depreciates at a rate of $(1 - \beta_1)$. When P exceeds o, new capital is added, and the initial level of housing services depends on the degree to which P exceeds o, on the relative cost of capital inputs $(\rho + \tau + \mu)$, and on the responsiveness of housing service supply to the addition of new capital (β_2). The β_2 parameter reflects a number of underlying factors, including producers' discount rates and expectations about the rate at which $P - o$ will decay over time. Both supply response parameters, β_1 and β_2, are estimated by fitting the model to historical data.[8]

New Construction

It is assumed that over a period as long as seven to ten years, the residential building industry will produce an unlimited quantity of new housing at an exogenous price per unit of housing services (P^*).[9] In effect, this assumption implies that any household has the option of commissioning the construction of a new dwelling and that, if it does so, it can consume any quantity of services at a constant price per unit of services. The only limitation on this perfectly elastic new dwelling supply function is that zoning and building codes are assumed to require that each new dwelling provide a minimum level of services (Q_{min}). Thus if a household chooses a quantity of housing services less than Q_{min}, it will not be eligible for a new dwelling.

For each market simulated by the model, the unit price of new housing services is established exogenously as the sum of the price of operating inputs and the price of new capital inputs. Thus

$$P^* = o^* + (\rho + \tau + \mu),$$

based on the assumption that for the marginal producer, profits are zero and the input prices for operations and capital are equal to the output price of housing services. Referring back to the profit function for the owner of an existing dwelling, we can express the unit price of existing housing services in similar terms. For the marginal producer, with zero profits, input prices for operations and capital are equal to the market price of housing services:

$$P = o + (\rho + \tau + \mu).$$

---

8. See de Leeuw and Struyk, *The Web of Urban Housing*, chapters 4 and 5.
9. For evidence on this point, see J.R. Follain, Jr., "The Price Elasticity of Long-Run Supply of New Housing Construction," *Land Economics*, vol. 55, no. 2 (May 1979), pp. 190-199.

The only difference between the unit prices of services realized by the marginal supplier of existing housing services and the unit prices of services realized by the marginal supplier of new housing services is the difference in the price of operating inputs. We assume that new dwellings are less costly to operate than existing dwellings are. The price of capital inputs, on the other hand, is assumed to be the same for new and existing dwellings. This assumption corresponds to our earlier assumption that prices of new capital inputs are the same as prices of originally invested inputs. In effect, a new dwelling is made up entirely of new capital inputs (plus operating inputs) with no existing capital to start with.

Household Demand

Each household in the metropolitan area bases its consumption of housing services on a utility function and a budget constraint. The utility derived by a household from a particular dwelling is a function of the quantity of housing services consumed (Q), the quantity of other goods consumed (X), and the characteristics of the neighborhood in which the dwelling is located (Z). This Stone-Geary utility function takes the form

$$U = (Q - \gamma_1 Q^*)^\alpha (X - \gamma_1 X^*)^{1-\alpha} Z_1 Z_2 Z_3, \quad 1 > \gamma_1 > 0.$$

The terms $\gamma_1 Q^*$ and $\gamma_1 X^*$ represent minimum acceptable quantities of housing services and other goods, calculated as a fraction (γ_1) of the quantities of housing services and other goods the household would consume in a new dwelling. As discussed later in the section on the solution process, each model household implicitly determines the quantity of housing and other goods it would consume in a new dwelling before it considers any of the existing model dwellings. Thus all existing dwellings are evaluated in relation to new dwelling services, which are available in unlimited quantities at the constant price, P^*.

The product of Z_1, Z_2, and Z_3 represents utility derived from the employment accessibility, relative wealth, and racial composition of the zone in which the dwelling is located. This utility function assumes that demand is separable in externalities; for any given dwelling, the optimum quantity of housing services demanded by a household is independent of neighborhood characteristics. Neighborhood characteristics are only important when a household compares one dwelling with another. For ease of exposition, these three terms are discussed further in the section on the solution process.

For any particular dwelling, a model household will consume the quantity of housing services that maximizes the partial utility term

$$u = (Q - \gamma_1 Q^*)^\alpha (X - \gamma_1 X^*)^{1-\alpha},$$

Appendix A

subject to a budget constraint.[10] In general terms, a household's budget constraint limits its expenditures on housing and other goods to its disposable income. As discussed earlier, the Urban Institute Model assumes that federal tax benefits for both rental and owner-occupied housing reduce the demand price of housing services perceived by the consumer. Thus the unit price upon which a household bases its consumption decision (P') differs from the market price upon which an owner bases production decisions (P). Both landlords and owner-occupants, in their role as producers, charge the same gross price, P. Neither renters nor owners, acting as consumers, actually pay P. Instead, they pay P'; and the derivation of P' depends upon a household's tenure, and, for owners, upon the choice of deduction method in paying income taxes. To complicate matters still further, disposable income also varies by tenure and tax deduction method. Before launching into a complete explanation of effective prices and disposable incomes, we can derive the household demand function in general terms, letting P' represent the effective service price perceived by a household and letting Y_D represent the household's after-tax disposable income.

The household budget constraint sets housing expenditures ($P'Q$) plus expenditures on other goods (X) equal to disposable income:

$$P'Q + X = Y_D,$$

and every household chooses levels of housing and other goods consumption (Q and X) that maximize utility (u) subject to this constraint. In a new dwelling—where, by definition, $P = P^*$, $Q = Q^*$, and $X = X^*$—maximizing u subject to the budget constraint yields

$$Q^* = \alpha Y_D / P^{*'},$$

and

$$X^* = (1 - \alpha) Y_D.$$

In an existing dwelling,

$$Q = \alpha(Y_D - \gamma_1 X^*)/P' + (1 - \alpha)\gamma_1 Q^*, \text{ and}$$

$$X = (1 - \alpha)(Y_D - \gamma_1 PQ^*) + \alpha \gamma_1 X^*.$$

The γ_1 parameter, which essentially reflects household responsiveness to changes in prices, is estimated by fitting the model to historical data. The α parameter, which reflects a household's preference for housing relative

---

10. This Stone-Geary utility function implies unitary price and income elasticities. In calibrating the model, we adjusted the income data so that the effective income elasticity is somewhat less than 1.0.

to other goods, is estimated from exogenous data on housing expense to income ratios.

Owner-Occupants' Housing Prices and Disposable Incomes

The next several paragraphs focus on households that own their own dwellings and provide expressions for the effective, after-tax price of housing services (P') and for disposable income (Y_D). Federal tax provisions allow owner-occupants to deduct mortgage interest and property taxes from their taxable income. However, to benefit from these deductions, a household must itemize all its deductions rather than claim the standard deduction. The Urban Institute Model assumes that households choose the deduction method that maximizes utility. Therefore, levels of housing services and other goods consumption are calculated for both deduction methods, so that the optimal method can be applied.

In addition to tax deductions, owner-occupants benefit from another price reduction generally not passed on to renter households. Owner-occupants as consumers ultimately realize the full value of their dwellings' appreciation. Rental properties also appreciate, but landlords cannot actually collect appreciation benefits in cash until the time of sale. Because capital gains are not realized on an accrual basis, it seems unlikely that landlords typically pass on appreciation benefits to their tenants, and we treat appreciation as an effective subsidy to the owner-occupant as consumer.[11] While owners, too, must wait until the time of sale to realize appreciation income, they clearly do realize the total benefit at that time and generally count appreciation as one of the economic incentives for homeownership. Thus before even considering the impacts of owner-occupant tax benefits, we subtract appreciation benefits (VQ) from the market price of housing services.[12]

---

11. One could argue that, for the same reason landlords are expected to pass tax benefits on to renter households, they can also be expected to pass on appreciation benefits. We reject this argument for two basic reasons. First, empirical data on landlord costs and revenues collected as part of the Housing Assistance Supply Experiment indicate that average rent revenues approximately equal the sum of operating, interest, property tax, and depreciation costs. If accrued appreciation benefits were passed on, observed rents would be considerably lower, perhaps low enough to yield a negative cash flow. This leads to our second reason for maintaining that appreciation benefits are not passed on to renters. Real estate investors are known to expect tax benefits in lieu of large annual cash returns from rental projects, but few investors are willing to contribute cash annually in anticipation of future appreciation benefits. In other words, a typical landlord will not accept a negative cash flow. See K. Neels, *Revenue and Expense Accounts for Rental Properties* (Santa Monica, Calif.: The Rand Corporation, 1982) and Touche Ross and Company, *Study on Tax Considerations in Multifamily Investment* (Washington, D.C.: U.S. Department of Housing and Urban Development, 1972).

12. In fact, only a fraction (10 percent) of the observed value of appreciation is subtracted from the price of housing services, since households do not value uncertain future benefits on a par with current costs.

Appendix A

Demand calculations are simplest when owner-occupant households claim the standard deduction, because the effective price of housing services faced by the household as a consumer is unaffected by taxes. In other words,

$$P' = P - V = o + (\rho + \tau + \mu - V)$$

for owner-occupants who claim the standard deduction. Disposable income (Y_D) for these households is equal to actual income (Y) less taxes (T).

Under the progressive federal tax system, a different marginal tax rate (t_b) is associated with each income bracket, where the subscript b identifies the bracket, and I_b identifies the lower boundary of the bracket. Each dollar of taxable income is taxed at the marginal rate for the bracket in which that dollar falls. Thus if I represents a household's taxable income, and if $I_b < I < I_{b+1}$, then

$$T = t_b(I - I_b) + t_{b-1}(I_{b-1} - I_{b-2}) + t_{b-2}(I_{b-2} - I_{b-3})\ldots,$$

or, in shortened form,

$$T = t_b(I - I_b) + T\{I_{b-1}\}.$$

In other words, taxes are calculated by multiplying the highest marginal tax rate (t_b) by the amount of taxable income falling in the b tax bracket ($I - I_b$) and then adding the taxes due on all income in lower brackets ($T\{I_{b-1}\}$).

Taxable income (I) for the owner-occupant household that claims the standard deduction is equal to actual income less exemptions (EX) and the standard deduction (STD). Thus

$$Y_D = Y - T$$

$$= Y - t_b(Y - EX - STD - I_b) - T\{I_{b-1}\}.$$

Owner-occupants who itemize their income tax deductions reduce the price they pay for housing services by deducting mortgage interest payments and property taxes from their taxable income. Taxable income (I) for owners who itemize can be expressed as

$$I = Y - EX - NHD - (\rho + \tau)Q.$$

where *NHD* represents a household's itemized nonhousing deductions, and the term $(\rho + \tau)Q$ represents mortgage interest and property tax payments. Thus taxes can be expressed as

$$T = t_b(Y - EX - NHD - (\rho + \tau)Q - I_b) + T\{I_{b-1}\}.$$

To derive the effective price of housing services (P') and disposable income (Y_D), we begin by setting the owner-occupant's *gross* housing expenditures (PQ) plus other goods expenditures equal to gross income less taxes ($Y - T$), where gross housing expenditures consist of operating costs, interest, property taxes, and real depreciation. Thus

$$oQ + (\rho + \tau + \mu - V)Q + X = Y - t_b(Y - EX - NHD \\ - (\rho + \tau)Q - I_b) \\ - T\{I_{b-1}\}.$$

Now if we collect all the terms that depend upon the level of housing consumption (Q), this budget constraint can be restated as

$$oQ + ((1 - t_b)(\rho + \tau) + \mu - V)Q + X = Y - t_b(Y - EX - NHD - I_b) \\ - T\{I_{b-1}\}.$$

Thus the net after-tax price paid by an owner-occupant who itemizes as the consumer of housing services is

$$P' = oQ + ((1 - t_b)(\rho + \tau) + \mu - V)Q,$$

and the corresponding disposable income term is

$$Y_D = Y - t_b(Y - EX - NHD - I_b) - T\{I_{b-1}\}.$$

Renters' Housing Prices and Disposable Incomes

Households that rent their dwellings cannot deduct any portion of their housing expenditures from taxable income. Therefore a renter household's federal tax calculation merely reduces disposable income, without affecting the price of housing services. However, the owners of rental real estate can claim tax deductions that are substantially greater than the tax breaks available from alternative investment opportunities. Because the calculation of these deductions has changed as a result of the Economic Recovery Tax Act of 1981 (ERTA), it is particularly important that the Urban Institute Model reflect the impact of investor tax benefits on rental housing supply and demand. In the 1970s, rental real estate could be de-

Appendix A

preciated for tax purposes at an accelerated rate exceeding the actual economic costs of depreciation. As a result of ERTA, the capital recovery period, or useful life, of rental real estate has been reduced, which further accelerates allowable depreciation deductions.

In effect, both before and after ERTA, landlords have received a subsidy from the Internal Revenue Service approximately equal to the difference between actual depreciation costs and allowable depreciation deductions. For a typical rental project of the 1970s, this difference was approximated at 5 percent of gross rents. Most investment analysts maintain that, in the long term, the special tax benefits available to rental housing relative to competing investment opportunities are passed on to renter households in the form of reduced rents. In the context of a long-term model, therefore, these tax benefits do not raise producer profits; instead, they reduce tenant rents. Thus if the term σ represents the magnitude of tax benefits to real estate investment, we can express a renter household's effective price of housing services as

$$P' = (1 - \sigma)P.$$

As stated earlier, a renter household's individual tax calculation does influence disposable income. A renter household's taxable income (I) is equal to its gross income (Y) less exemptions and either the standard deduction or itemized nonhousing deductions, whichever is greater. Thus the renter household's disposable income can be calculated as

$$Y_D = Y - t_b(Y - EX - max(STD, NHD) - I_b) - T\{I_{b-1}\}.$$

Solution Process

Given the behavioral rules governing households, housing service suppliers, and the building industry, the Urban Institute Model is solved by allocating model households to a metropolitan area's model dwellings. A model solution is characterized by three basic conditions. First, each household is consuming the quantity of housing services and paying the market price that represent the intersection of household demand and dwelling supply for the dwelling it occupies. Second, no household would prefer a dwelling over the one to which it has been assigned for which the market price is lower than what the household would pay. In other words, a household may not necessarily be assigned to the dwelling it most prefers, but all dwellings that offer greater utility are occupied by households that pay higher unit prices than the household would pay. Third, neighborhood characteristics that result from the allocation of model households to model dwellings, specifically, racial composition and relative wealth, must correspond to the assumed neighborhood characteristics upon which the allocation is based.

These three conditions are satisfied by a four-step solution process. These steps are outlined here and then discussed in more depth in the remainder of this section. First, the micro-equilibrium level of housing consumption for every model household in every model dwelling is determined. Next, the utility derived by each household from every available dwelling is calculated, based on assumed (i.e., exogenously assigned) neighborhood characteristics. The third step in the solution process allocates model households to model dwellings, assigning each household to its most preferred dwelling and resolving conflicts between households in favor of the household offering the highest price. Finally, after all households have been allocated, the resulting neighborhood characteristics are evaluated. If these characteristics differ from the assumed neighborhood characteristics upon which the allocation was based, then the original assumptions are adjusted to correspond to the characteristics implied by the latest allocation, utility values are recalculated for each household in each dwelling, and the allocation process is repeated. In effect, one can think of the assumed characteristics as those actually present at the start of the simulation period; in the first full solution iteration households respond to these, but in later iterations they respond to those reflecting the sorting of households to locations over the period.

The first step in the Urban Institute Model solution process is to determine micro-equilibrium levels of housing and other goods consumption for every model household in every model dwelling. Micro-equilibrium consumption levels are determined by calculating the intersection of the household demand function,

$$Q = \alpha(Y_D - \gamma_1 X^*)/P' + (1 - \alpha)\gamma_1 Q^*,$$

and the existing dwelling supply function,

$$Q = [\beta_1 + \beta_2(P - o)/(\rho + \tau + \mu)]Q_o,$$

where P represents the market price upon which supply behavior is based, and P' represents the effective price upon which demand behavior is based.

The intersection of dwelling supply and household demand is calculated by substituting the supply function into the demand function and solving the resulting quadratic for the market price, P. Thus P is the posi-

Appendix A

tive root of the equation $aP^2 + bP + c = 0$, where the values of the coefficients a, b, and c vary with tenure and deduction method. For renters,

$a = \beta_2 Q_o/(\rho + \tau + \mu)$,
$b = \beta_1 Q_o - \beta_2 Q_o o/(\rho + \tau + \mu) - (1 - \alpha)\gamma_1 Q^*$,
$c = -(\alpha/(1 - \sigma))(Y_D - \gamma_1 X^*)$.

For owners who claim the standard deduction,

$a = \beta_2 Q_o/(\rho + \tau + \mu)$,
$b = \beta_1 Q_o - \beta_2 Q_o(o + V)/(\rho + \tau + \mu) - (1 - \alpha)\gamma_1 Q^*$,
$c = VQ_o(\beta_2 o/(\rho + \tau + \mu) - \beta_1) - \alpha(Y_D - \gamma_1 X^*)$
$\quad + (1 - \alpha)\gamma_1 VQ^*$.

For owners who itemize deductions,

$a = \beta_2 Q_o/(\rho + \tau + \mu)$,
$b = \beta_1 Q_o - \beta_2 Q_o(o + t_b(\rho + \tau) + V)/(\rho + \tau + \mu) - (1 - \alpha)\gamma_1 Q^*$,
$c = (t_b(\rho + \tau) + V)Q_o(\beta_2 o/(\rho + \tau + \mu) - \beta_1) - \alpha(Y_D - \gamma_1 X^*) +$
$\quad (t_b(\rho + \tau) + V)(1 - \alpha)\gamma_1 Q^*$.

Once we have solved for the market value of P, the corresponding level of housing services (Q) that maximizes both household utility and producer profit is calculated by simply substituting P into the household demand function. Then, the household's implied consumption of other goods (X) is determined by substituting both P and Q into the household's budget constraint.

This micro-equilibrium solution step is repeated for every model household in every model dwelling. Thus when the first stage of the solution process is complete, we know the quantity of housing and other goods each household would consume and the market price it would pay for each model dwelling. There is one exception to this general statement: potentially, a household's demand curve may not intersect with a particular dwelling's supply curve. Specifically, to ensure a valid intersection, P must be greater than or equal to o, Q must be greater than or equal to $\gamma_1 Q^*$, and X must be greater than or equal to $\gamma_1 X^*$. In other words, the market price of housing services must cover operating costs, and levels of housing and other goods consumption must meet the household's minimum standards.

To calculate intersections of household demand functions and existing dwelling supply functions, the model must generate the quantity of housing and the quantity of other goods each household would consume in a new dwelling (Q^* and X^*) at the constant unit price P^*. As long as Q^* exceeds the government-imposed minimum on new dwelling quality (Q_{min}), the intersection between household demand and new dwelling supply is valid.

The second step in the solution process involves the calculation of total utility derived by every household from every available dwelling. As discussed earlier, household utility (U) is defined as

$$U = (Q - \gamma_1 Q^*)^\alpha (X - \gamma_1 X^*)^{1-\alpha} Z_1 Z_2 Z_3.$$

The first two terms in this expression, which measure utility derived from housing consumption and other goods consumption, are by-products of the micro-equilibrium solutions discussed earlier. The product $Z_1 Z_2 Z_3$ represents the level of utility derived from a neighborhood's employment accessibility, relative wealth, and racial composition. We now discuss the specification of each of these terms.

Neighborhood accessibility is given exogenously in terms of the average number of leisure hours per month remaining after commuting to work ($200 - H$), and a sensitivity parameter (λ). Utility derived from accessibility (Z_1) is expressed as

$$Z_1 = (200 - H)\lambda.$$

The λ parameter varies both by household and by zone and is derived by equating two expressions for the marginal cost of commuting ($\delta Y/\delta H$). The first of these two expressions reflects the assumption that households value their commuting time at approximately half their hourly wage rate and work 170 hours per month.[13] Thus

$$\delta Y/\delta H = -0.5 w Y/170,$$

where w is the fraction of monthly income accounted for by wages. The second expression for $\delta Y/\delta H$ is derived from the model's utility function,

$$\delta Y/\delta H = -\lambda(1 - \gamma_1) Y/((1 - \gamma_1) + \gamma_1 \alpha)(200 - H).$$

Equating these two expressions and solving for λ yields

$$\lambda = 0.00294 w (1 - \gamma_1 + \gamma_1 \alpha)(200 - H)/(1 - \gamma_1).$$

---

13. For evidence on this point, see P.R. Stopher and A.H. Meyburg, *Transportation Systems Evaluation* (Lexington, Mass.: D.C. Heath and Co., 1976), pp. 37–66.

Appendix A

Neighborhood racial composition and relative wealth are ultimately determined by the allocation of model households to model dwellings. Therefore, the model starts with assumed neighborhood race and wealth characteristics and then adjusts them after examining the resulting allocation of model households.

The wealth term is included in the model to account for the fact that Americans have historically exhibited a desire for socially homogeneous residential environments. In the context of exclusionary local zoning practices, economists have acknowledged the existence of these preferences and have attempted to specify their equity and efficiency implications.[14] However, few analyses have attempted to address the broader phenomenon of moderate segregation—on the basis of income and education, for example—*within* jurisdictions that accompanies more dramatic differences *between* jurisdictions.[15]

Because so little work has been done to document the strength and form of households' preferences for social homogeneity, the model's specification of this term is necessarily rather arbitrary. The relative wealth of a zone (R) is approximated by the ratio of average housing expenditures within the zone to average expenditures in the metropolitan area as a whole. All households are assumed to prefer wealthier neighborhoods, such that

$$Z_2 = R^{0.01}\gamma_2,$$

where γ_2 is a calibrated parameter.

Residential segregation on the basis of race and discrimination against blacks in housing markets are facts of American urban life that must be reflected in the model.[16] A series of recent papers provides the basis for our treatment of the effect of the racial composition of a zone on the utility derived by a household from a particular dwelling. Conceptual models by Courant and Kern show that preferences on the part of whites to sell to other whites impose higher search costs on blacks, which in turn

---

14. For a general review, see W. Fischel, "Equity and Efficiency Aspects of Zoning Reform," *Public Policy*, vol. 27, no. 3 (summer 1979), pp. 301–332.

15. Farley presents segregation indices of this type; see R. Farley, "Residential Segregation in Urbanized Areas of the United States in 1970: An Analysis of Social Class and Racial Differences," *Demography*, vol. 14, no. 4 (Nov. 1977), pp. 497–518. Also, such preferences have been demonstrated in various analyses with hedonic indices. For example, for Boston and Pittsburgh, see A. Schnare and R. Struyk, "An Analysis of Ghetto Housing Prices Over Time," in G. Ingram, ed., *Residential Location and Urban Housing Markets* (Cambridge, Mass.: Ballinger, 1977), pp. 95–134.

16. For evidence on the extent of discrimination, see R. Wienk, C. Reid, J. Simonson, and F. Eggers, *Measuring Racial Discrimination in American Housing Markets: The Housing Market Practices Survey* (Washington, D.C.: U.S. Department of Housing and Urban Development, 1979).

raise the price of housing within black areas.[17] The same result is obtained if both blacks and whites prefer to live in white neighborhoods, but the preferences of whites in this regard are stronger than those of blacks.

The idea that blacks prefer to live in racially mixed areas is supported by various opinion surveys[18] and by careful empirical studies. Yinger, in his reanalysis of St. Louis data, specified racial composition as a neighborhood amenity and found that as the percentage of blacks increases, the unit price of housing declines in predominantly white areas but rises in black and integrated areas.[19] Similarly, Galster, in an analysis of the St. Louis data and additional data for Wooster, Ohio, concluded that whites have a strong preference to live in exclusively or predominantly white areas.[20] He also found that black owners in St. Louis had an aversion to living in predominantly black neighborhoods in comparison with predominantly white neighborhoods.

In light of these various findings, the specification in the utility function is that whites have a preference for living with whites and that blacks are race neutral. This is consistent with the broad conclusion of the studies reviewed that whites have stronger preferences to live with whites than blacks do.

For whites,

$$Z_3 = PRPWHT + (1000/(100\ \gamma_3 + 1)),$$

where *PRPWHT* is the percentage of all households in a zone that are white, γ_3 is a calibrated parameter. For blacks, $Z_3 = 1.0$.

This form requires a word of explanation. The simplest form would be *PRPWHT* raised to some exponent, but this is unacceptable, as it would make utility zero in many cases. With the form chosen, Z_3 is never equal to zero, and increases in γ_3 are associated with increases in racial prejudice or discrimination. With $\gamma_3 = 0$, Z_3 can vary only between 1,000 and 1,001, a

---

17. P.N. Courant, "Racial Prejudice in a Search Model of the Urban Housing Market," *Journal of Urban Economics*, vol. 5, no. 3 (July 1978), pp. 329-345; C.R. Kern, "Racial Prejudice and Residential Segregation: The Yinger Model Revisited," *Journal of Urban Economics*, vol. 10, no. 2 (September 1981), pp. 164-172.

18. T. Pettigrew, "Attitudes on Race and Housing: A Social Psychological View," in A. Hawley and U. Rock, eds., *Segregation in Residential Areas* (Washington, D.C.: National Academy of Sciences, 1973); H. Schuman and S. Hatchett, *Black Racial Attitudes* (Ann Arbor, Mich.: University of Michigan Press, 1974); D. Davis and E. Casett, "Do Black Students Want to Live in Integrated Socially Homogeneous Neighborhoods?" *Economic Geography*, vol. 54, no. 2 (July 1978), pp. 197-209.

19. J. Yinger, "The Black-White Price Differential in Housing: Some Further Evidence," *Land Economics*, vol. 54, no. 2 (May 1978), pp. 188-208.

20. G.C. Galster, "Black and White Preferences for Neighborhood Racial Composition," *American Real Estate and Urban Economics Association Journal*, vol. 10, no. 1 (spring 1982), pp. 39-66.

Appendix A

range of only 0.1 percent of total utility. With $\gamma_3 = 1$, Z_3 can vary between approximately 10 and 11, a range of about 10 percent.

In the third step of the Urban Institute Model solution process, model households are allocated to model dwellings, based on the utility they derive from alternative dwellings and on the unit prices they are willing to pay for housing services. The allocation step is accomplished by considering one model household at a time, starting with households that exhibit the greatest αY values. The model first attempts to allocate a household to its most preferred dwelling. If that dwelling is vacant, or if it is a new dwelling, the household under consideration occupies it, and the model moves on to consider the next household. If, on the other hand, a household's preferred dwelling is already occupied, then the model compares the micro-equilibrium market price offered by the current occupant to the micro-equilibrium market price offered by the unallocated household under consideration. The household that offers the higher micro-equilibrium price wins the competition for the dwelling, and the loser household must consider its next most preferred dwelling. The loser household does not reassess the utility that might be derived from the dwelling at the higher unit price. If the household's micro-equilibrium price does not win the bidding competition, the household must consider the next most preferred dwelling. This process is repeated until all households have been allocated.

Once the allocation is complete, the model performs the final step in the solution process, comparing assumed neighborhood wealth and racial characteristics with the actual characteristics implied by the allocation of model households to model dwellings. If the implied characteristics differ from the assumptions upon which the allocation was based, then the assumptions are adjusted, utility values are recalculated, and the households are reallocated according to the procedure just outlined.

APPENDIX B

GENERATING THE DATA FOR MODEL SOLUTIONS

To date, all implementations of the Urban Institute Model have relied upon data derived primarily from 1960 and 1970 Census publications. The current implementation is the first to employ entirely new data sets, obtained primarily from the national Annual Housing Survey (AHS) tapes for 1973 and 1980. The model is calibrated for the period 1973-1980. Since the solution period must remain the same, policy simulations extend from 1980 through 1987. The level of detail available from the AHS tapes regarding household and dwelling characteristics is considerably richer than what was available from decennial Census publications. Therefore, we have been able to improve upon many of the procedures used to generate earlier Urban Institute Model data sets. This discussion compares the data collection procedures employed in the current implementation with the original procedures outlined in *The Web of Urban Housing*.[1]

Earlier Urban Institute Model data sets have characterized both actual and prototypical metropolitan areas and have generally distinguished four to six geographic zones within each area. In the current implementation, we calibrate the model and conduct policy simulations for two "prototypical" metropolitan areas, representing the average of metropolitan areas in the Northeast and West Census regions. The AHS does not provide sufficient geographic information to identify as many as four to six neighborhoods or zones in each area. Moreover, the relevance of so many zones to national policy analysis is limited. Therefore, only two zones are identified in each region's prototypical SMSA: central city and suburbs.[2]

---

1. F. de Leeuw and R. Struyk, *The Web of Urban Housing: Analyzing Policy with a Market Simulation Model* (Washington, D.C.: The Urban Institute Press, 1975).

2. In generating zonal data for each regional prototype, we are limited to metropolitan areas in which central city and suburban dwellings are distinguished. Thus the regional averages exclude SMSAs for which the AHS has not identified dwellings' locations. Control totals are derived from published data on all metropolitan areas in the two regions.

The remainder of this appendix focuses in considerable detail upon the Urban Institute Model's various data requirements and consists of three major sections. The first section describes the procedures employed to generate data for calibrating the model for the 1973-1980 period. The second section then outlines calibration procedures and presents the calibration results. Finally, the third section discusses assumptions and procedures used to generate data for the 1980-1987 simulations.

Calibration Data, 1973-1980

The Urban Institute Model calibration process consists of two phases. In the first phase, demand parameters are calibrated by solving the model for a single year, in this case, 1973. This solution allocates a metropolitan area's 1973 population across the 1973 housing stock. No new construction or changes in the supply of services from existing dwelling units occurs. The second phase calibrates supply parameters by solving the model for the full 1973-1980 period. The initial 1973 housing stock is modified by new construction and by changes in the level of housing services provided by existing dwellings. Then the metropolitan area's 1980 population is allocated across this modified housing stock. Thus for calibration purposes, the Urban Institute Model's primary inputs are (1) characteristics of the housing stock in 1973, (2) determinants of the price of housing services, (3) characteristics of new construction, and (4) characteristics of the metropolitan area's population in both 1973 and 1980. We discuss each of these major inputs in turn and then present data on subsidized housing units, income tax rates, and commuting costs.

The Housing Stock, 1973

The first step in characterizing a metropolitan area's housing stock is to observe the level of housing expenditures (PQ) in every dwelling and to convert these expenditure levels into location-free quantity measures. The original strategy employed in *The Web of Urban Housing* consisted of four steps. First, regression equations were estimated relating rents and values to dwelling attributes and to location. Second, the estimated coefficients were applied to the average dwelling characteristics for each zone, and location variables were set to SMSA averages rather than zonal averages. This step produced location-free estimates of each zone's average rents (R) and values (V). In the third step, rent to value ratios (R/V) were applied to obtain rental equivalents for owner-occupied housing for which only V is reported. Then each zone's overall average housing expenditures ($\widetilde{PQ}$) and estimated location-free housing expenditures ($\widetilde{PQ}$) were computed. Fi-

Appendix B

nally, a price deflator for each zone was calculated as $\widetilde{PQ}/\widehat{PQ}$. This price deflator ($P_k$) represents the unit price of housing services in zone k, where units of Q have been defined such that the unit price of housing services in the metropolitan area's average dwelling is 1.0. For any dwelling, then, the quantity of housing services (Q) can be computed as PQ/P_k.[3]

We have adopted this basic strategy with one significant modification. Instead of converting owner-occupant house values to rents by means of an average R/V ratio, we impute owner-occupant housing expenditures using a hedonic equation estimated from observed renter housing expenditures. For each region, the hedonic equation expresses expenditures (PQ) as a function of dwelling and neighborhood characteristics. This hedonic equation is estimated for renter-occupied dwellings and is then applied to impute PQ values for owner-occupied units as well as for vacant units, households paying no cash rent, and households not reporting their rent.[4] Table B.1 identifies the variables included in this specification and presents the estimated parameter values for the prototypical metropolitan areas.

Using a hedonic equation to impute owner-occupant expenditures reflects an assumption that owner-occupants face essentially the same housing production costs as do the landlords of comparable rental units. This assumption is embodied in the Urban Institute Model's theoretical framework, which applies the same housing service production function to both owner-occupied and rental housing. However, our theoretical framework requires that we adjust observed rents slightly before treating them as analogous to owner-occupied housing expenditures. Specifically, observed rents are actually lower than the rent revenues realized by landlords, because of the impact of tax benefits passed on to housing service consumers. Therefore, observed rents must be adjusted upward to reflect the actual, unsubsidized price of housing services.[5]

Once we have an observed or imputed PQ value for every dwelling—excluding government-subsidized and public housing units—we can apply the basic strategy employed in *The Web of Urban Housing* to calculate central city and suburban price deflators. First, we apply the estimated coefficients from the hedonic equation to the average dwelling characteristics for each zone, setting location characteristics to the SMSA averages rather than the zonal averages. This yields location-free estimates of average zonal expenditures ($\widehat{PQ}$). Then the price deflator for each zone is cal-

---

3. F. de Leeuw and R. Struyk, *The Web of Urban Housing*.
4. J.R. Follain, Jr., and S. Malpezzi, "Dissecting Housing Value and Rent: Estimates on Hedonic Indexes for Thirty-Nine SMSAs," Working Paper 249-17 (Washington, D.C.: The Urban Institute, 1979).
5. Before enactment of ERTA in 1981, accelerated depreciation benefits were estimated as amounting to about 5 percent of rents. Thus observed PQ equals 95 percent of actual PQ.

TABLE B.1

Housing Expenditure Hedonic Specification, 1973

Variable	Label	Northeast	West
LNBLT	Log of structure age	−0.1297**	−0.0931
LGAPT	Unit in building of 20 or more units	0.0358*	0.0251
SFDET	Single family detached unit	0.0494	0.0190
FLOORS	Number of floors	0.0891**	0.0785
ELEV	Unit in building with elevator	0.1625**	0.1811*
ROOMS	Number of rooms	0.0428**	0.0008
BEDRMS	Number of bedrooms	0.0795**	0.1782**
CELEC	Cooking fuel is electricity	−0.0276	0.0321
NUMBTHS	Number of bathrooms	0.2602**	0.1426**
HELEC	Heating fuel is electricity	0.1790**	0.0270
CENFURN	Unit has central furnace	0.1034**	0.0712**
BADHEAT	Unit has inadequate heating equipment	−0.0655	0.0578*
STMHEAT	Unit heated with steam	0.1885**	0.0180
COLD	Rooms unheated in winter	−0.0424	0.0591**
CENAIR	Unit has central air conditioner	0.1020**	0.0637*
CELLAR	Unit has cellar	0.0186	0.0082
CRACKS	Cracks in walls, ceiling	−0.0001	−0.0731*
PLASTER	Holes in plaster	0.0046	−0.0302
PRIV	Rooms lacking privacy	−0.1069**	−0.0744**
BADHALL	Deficiencies in common hallways	−0.0453**	−0.0332
RATESTR	Opinion of street	−0.0318**	−0.0557**
ABAN	Abandoned buildings on street	−0.0752**	−0.1537**
AIRNOIS	Presence of airplane noise	0.0202*	−0.0007
STRCRIM	Presence of street crime	0.0005	0.0104
STRNOIS	Presence of street noise	−0.0136	0.0124
STRTRAF	Presence of heavy traffic	0.0036	0.0112
BADSCHL	Neighborhood schools inadequate	0.0108	0.0511*
BADSHOP	Neighborhood shopping inadequate	−0.0369*	−0.0467**
CENCITY	Unit located in the central city	−0.0538**	0.0240
BLACK	Head of household black	−0.0215	0.0251
LENGTEN	Length of tenure	−0.0149**	−0.0091**
ZCROWD	Unit overcrowded	0.0927**	0.0033
constant		4.6768	4.7859
R^2		0.4352	0.5040

NOTE: * indicates significance at the 95 percent confidence level; ** indicates significance at the 99 percent confidence level.

culated as the ratio of actual average zonal rents ($\widetilde{PQ}$) to the location-free average. Thus the average price of housing services in a given zone, $P_k = \widetilde{PQ}/\widehat{PQ}$, and the resulting average value of P across zones for a given SMSA is 1.0. In other words, we have effectively defined our units of housing services (Q) such that the unit price of services offered by a prototypical SMSA's average dwelling is 1.0. Table B.2 presents the results of calculating price deflators for each regional prototype.

Appendix B

TABLE B.2
Monthly Housing Expenditures and Price Deflators, 1973

	Northeast	West
SMSA average PQ	$187	$196
Central city		
PQ	164	187
P_k	0.960	1.008
Suburbs		
PQ	207	202
P_k	1.034	0.994

Given observed or imputed PQ values for every dwelling, and given the zonal price deflators, we compute the quantity of housing services offered by each metropolitan area dwelling. Then we construct a representative distribution of model dwellings, using essentially the same techniques as those employed in *The Web of Urban Housing*. For each dwelling in the metropolitan area, we calculate a beginning-of-period level of housing services by dividing housing expenditures by the applicable zonal price deflator ($Q = PQ/P_k$). Next, dwellings located in the central city and dwellings located in the suburbs are sorted on the basis of levels of housing services. Assisted dwellings—both those in public housing projects and those whose occupants receive government rent subsidies—are excluded from the resulting sorted lists. Finally, the two sorted dwelling distributions are collapsed into model dwellings, using a ratio of model to actual dwellings chosen to yield approximately seventy-five model dwellings per prototypical metropolitan area. Thus each model dwelling is assigned an initial level of housing services (Q_o) equal to the average service levels of a range of actual dwellings. Table B.3 presents the number of model dwellings in each prototypical SMSA for both central city and suburban zones.

Determining the Price of Housing Services

Incorporating owner-occupant income tax provisions into the Urban Institute Model framework requires that we distinguish the prices of operations (o), interest (ρ), property taxes (τ), and depreciation (μ) that make up the price of housing services (P). In addition, a measure of dwelling appreciation is required in order to simulate the net effective price of housing services to owner-occupants.[6] We begin by presenting initial, beginning-of-decade values and then estimate average values for the 1973–1980 period.

---

6. See appendix A.

TABLE B.3

NUMBER OF MODEL DWELLINGS, 1973

	Northeast	West
Central city	34	33
Suburbs	42	41
Total	76	74

The Housing Allowance Supply Experiment has generated an unusually detailed sample of data on the costs incurred by owners of rental units.[7] We use average expenditures for detailed expense categories constructed from 1973 Green Bay data to estimate the proportionate share of housing expenditures attributable to operations, interest, property taxes, and depreciation. As indicated earlier, the use of data on rental properties is reasonable if we assume that owner-occupants face essentially the same production costs as do the landlords of comparable rental units.

Table B.4 identifies the expenditure categories corresponding to each of our housing production cost components, presents average annual expenditures for Green Bay, and calculates each component's proportionate share of total housing expenditures. Because our units of Q have been defined such that $P = 1.0$ in the average dwelling, the component price terms (o, ρ, τ, and μ) that make up the value of P can be expressed as 0.394, 0.244, 0.195, and 0.167, respectively, for both prototypical SMSAs.

The values of o, ρ, τ, and μ, estimated for 1973, reflect the costs of producing housing services in 1973, with capital inputs invested during or before 1973. These values are appropriate for the initial 1973 calibration runs. To simulate the full 1973-1980 period, we need average o, ρ, τ, and μ values for the seven years. These are calculated by using applicable rates of change to adjust the 1973 values.

The operating cost values (o) for the 1973-1980 simulation are estimated for each region by increasing the 1973 values by a factor calculated from the CPI fuels and other utilities index.[8] This factor is the ratio of the mean of the 1973-1980 annual indexes to the 1973 index. Table B.5 presents the results of these calculations for the two regions.

Table B.5 also presents the results of similar calculations for adjustments to the capital inputs prices, ρ, τ, and μ. To yield 1973-1980 prices,

---

7. K. Neels, *Revenue and Expense Accounts for Rental Properties* (Santa Monica, Calif.: The Rand Corporation, 1982).

8. Unfortunately, the CPI fuels and other utilities index does not capture all the elements of the operating inputs price (o). Specifically, o includes telephone, water, and sewer expenditures, as well as housekeeping supplies and equipment.

Appendix B

TABLE B.4
Average Annual Housing Production Costs for Green Bay, 1973

	Per Unit Expenditures (In dollars)	Proportion of Total
Operating costs (oQ)		
Insurance premiums and self-insurance	35	
Utility expenses	352	
Management expenses	104	
Other operating expenses	63	
Total	554	0.394
Other costs		
Mortgage interest payments (ρQ)	342	0.244
Property taxes and special assessments (τQ)	274	0.195
Capital maintenance expenses (μQ)	235	0.167
Implied PQ ($oQ + (\rho + \tau + \mu)Q$)	1,405	1.00

SOURCE: K. Neels, *Energy Use in Housing* (Santa Monica, Calif.: The Rand Corporation, 1983).

each 1973 price term is adjusted up by a factor that reflects the rate at which average prices over the decade exceeded the initial 1973 prices. Each adjustment factor (F) is calculated as:

$$F = \frac{I_{73}*W_{73} + I_{74}*W_{74} + \ldots I_{80}*W_{80}}{W_{73} + W_{74} + \ldots W_{80}} / I_{73},$$

where $I_{73}, I_{74}, \ldots I_{80}$ represent price index values for the years 1973-1980, and the weights $W_{73}, W_{74} \ldots W_{80}$ represent the proportion of all 1973 to 1980 new construction built in each year.[9]

For owner-occupants, the effective price of housing services—both in new dwellings and in existing dwellings—is reduced by the benefits of value appreciation (V). We estimate V on the basis of the average change in new single-family house prices exclusive of increases in construction

---

9. Number of newly constructed, year-round dwelling units inside SMSAs, by region. From U.S. Department of Commerce, Bureau of the Census, *Annual Housing Survey: 1973-1980, Part A, General Housing Characteristics for the U.S. and Regions* (Washington, D.C.: U.S. Government Printing Office).

TABLE B.5

HOUSING SERVICE PRICE COMPONENTS, 1973-1980

	Northeast	West
o-1973 value	0.394	0.394
Percentage change, 1973-1980 average	+58.86	+41.97
1973-1980 value	0.626	0.559
ρ-1973 value	0.244	0.244
Percentage change, 1973-1980 average[a]	24.9	24.9
1973-1980 value	0.305	0.305
τ-1973 value	0.195	0.195
Percentage change, 1973-1980 average[b]	−8.7	−34.8
1973-1980 value	0.179	0.127
μ-1973 value	0.167	0.167
Percentage change, 1973-1980 average[c]	+43.0	+50.2
1973-1980 value	0.239	0.251

SOURCES:

a. Federal Home Loan Bank Board new home mortgage yields, 1973-1980. In *Economic Report of the President 1981* (Washington, D.C.: U.S. Government Printing Office, 1981) p. 278.

b. Mean real estate taxes per $1,000 value, U.S. Department of Commerce, Bureau of the Census *Annual Housing Survey, Part C: Financial Characteristics of the Housing Inventory, 1973-1980* (Washington, D.C.: U.S. Government Printing Office).

c. Average Boeckh cost index numbers for frame residential construction, January and February, 1973-1980. Boeckh Publications, *Boeckh Building Cost Index Numbers* (Milwaukee, Wisc.: 1973-1980).

NOTE: All price terms are expressed in terms of the model's units of housing services.

costs over the 1973-1980 period.[10] We apply the resulting rates of increase to the average 1973 value of owner-occupied dwellings for each regional prototype.[11] This value is then converted into a monthly dollar benefit of appreciation for the average dwelling in each prototypical SMSA (VQ). Finally, to compute the per unit value of appreciation, we simply divide VQ by the quantity of housing services (Q) in the average dwelling for each prototypical SMSA. The results of these calculations are presented in table B.6.

---

10. Price index of new homes obtained from U.S. Bureau of Census, *Construction Reports*—"Price Index of New One-Family Homes Sold, 1973-1980" (Washington, D.C.: U.S. Department of Commerce). Change in residential construction costs obtained from Boeckh, "Construction Cost Index Numbers" frame residential structures, January to February 1972 and 1973. Share of price index attributable to construction costs obtained from U.S. Bureau of the Census, *Construction Reports*, "Characteristics of New One-Family Homes, 1973" (Washington, D.C.: U.S. Department of Commerce).

11. Median dwelling value, inside SMSAs, by region, from *Annual Housing Survey*.

Appendix B

TABLE B.6
1973–1980 Appreciation Benefits

	Northeast	West
Average value increase	31.3%	205.9%
Average dwelling value	$30,700	$29,100
VQ	$100	$624
Average Q	187	196
V	0.535	3.184

Characteristics of New Construction

The model assumes that a metropolitan area's construction industry will supply an unlimited quantity of new dwelling services at a fixed price $P* = o* + (\rho + \tau + \mu)$, where $o*$, ρ, τ, and μ represent average supply costs over the period rather than initial, beginning-of-period costs. For owner-occupants, the new construction price ($P*$) is reduced by appreciation benefits (V). Government regulations as well as other constraints are assumed to impose a minimum quantity of new dwelling services (Q_{min}) such that no new dwelling can be built unless the micro-equilibrium level of housing consumption exceeds Q_{min}.

Values of ρ, τ, and μ for the period 1973–1980 are assumed to apply to new as well as existing dwellings.[12] Operating costs, on the other hand, can be expected to be lower for new units than they are for existing units.

To estimate the 1973–1980 price of operating a new dwelling ($o*$), we adjust our o value for existing dwellings to reflect differences between new and existing units. The adjustment factor is derived from an energy usage regression that incorporates structure age as well as other structural and household characteristics.[13] The coefficients on age are multiplied by the average ages of new and existing units in each region.[14] The difference between these two products represents the percentage reduction in energy usage enjoyed by new construction. Table B.7 presents the results of these calculations.

The next task in the process of constructing new dwelling parameters is to estimate values of Q_{min}, the government-imposed minimum on new dwelling services. We assume that Q_{min} varies by tenure and zone. These values are derived from the PQ distribution for dwellings built since 1973 in the 1980 AHS, grouping these dwellings by tenure and zone. Values of

---

12. See appendix A.
13. K. Neels, *Energy Use in Housing* (Santa Monica, Calif.: The Rand Corporation, 1983).
14. Distribution of year built inside SMSAs by region, from *Annual Housing Survey*.

TABLE B.7

PRICE OF OPERATING INPUTS FOR NEW DWELLINGS, 1973-1980

	Northeast	West
1973-1980 o value	0.626	0.559
New dwelling discount	8.68%	6.96%
1973-1980 o^* value	0.572	0.520

Q are computed by dividing PQ by the price of new construction for the region. Table B.8 presents the resulting Q_{min} values.

Population Characteristics, 1973-1980

The 1973-1980 calibration data set requires that we construct two sets of model households for each prototypical SMSA, one representing metropolitan area population characteristics in 1973 and one representing the corresponding characteristics in 1980. Thus the process described here is performed once with 1973 AHS data and again with 1980 AHS data. To construct a metropolitan area population of model households, we employ generally the same procedures as those described in *The Web of Urban Housing*. However, after examining household distributions and expenditure patterns by race, tenure, age, and household composition, we arrived at a new set of household types: (1) white, elderly households; (2) white, nonelderly husband-wife households; (3) other nonelderly, white households, including single individuals and single heads of household; and (4) black households.

Each model household must be represented by a tenure designation and an actual income figure. For each household type, a set of model households is constructed from AHS data by means of a three-step process. First, all households of a given type are sorted in income order. Then, a ratio of actual households to model households is applied to collapse the

TABLE B.8

NEW CONSTRUCTION MINIMUMS

	Northeast	West
Central city		
Owners	180.98	268.01
Renters	160.88	206.16
Suburbs		
Owners	205.37	292.70
Renters	186.70	209.07

Appendix B

sorted income distribution. Thus if the ratio of actual to model households is 100, the poorest model household is constructed from the characteristics of the 100 poorest actual households. This process is analogous to the process employed to construct model dwellings from the sorted distributions of actual dwellings. Finally, each model household is assigned a tenure based on the tenure of the actual households represented by that model household. Table B.9 presents the distributions of model households by type and tenure for 1973 and 1980.

In addition to the household-specific data, demand behavior in the model is governed by some characteristics of the household types, including median incomes and α parameters, which measure the responsiveness of housing expenditures to variations in income. Median monthly income values are straightforwardly derived and are presented in Table B.10. The α parameters require further explanation.

In the Urban Institute Model, the α parameters reflect households' preferences for housing relative to other goods. In previous implementations, these parameters were approximated by average housing expense to income ratios for each household type.[15] We continue to treat housing expense to income ratios as an estimate of α, but we allow these values to vary by income as well as by household type. In other words, within a single household type, α declines as income rises. Before α functions can be estimated, gross housing expenditures and incomes must be adjusted, to reflect the impact of income taxes and appreciation on the effective price of

TABLE B.9

Numbers of Model Households, 1973 and 1980

Household Type	1973 Northeast	1973 West	1980 Northeast	1980 West
White, elderly				
Owners	9	7	9	8
Renters	6	4	4	3
White, nonelderly husband-wife				
Owners	29	30	29	33
Renters	11	11	9	11
White, nonelderly other				
Owners	5	6	7	12
Renters	9	11	13	19
Black				
Owners	2	2	3	2
Renters	5	3	6	4

---

15. F. de Leeuw and R. Struyk, *The Web of Urban Housing*.

TABLE B.10

MEDIAN MONTHLY INCOMES BY HOUSEHOLD TYPE AND TENURE
(IN DOLLARS)

	1973		1980	
Household Type	Northeast	West	Northeast	West
White, elderly				
Owners	427.00	444.83	786.50	889.83
Renters	382.00	305.67	548.67	550.00
White, nonelderly husband-wife				
Owners	1,255.00	1,291.67	2,294.67	2,506.46
Renters	913.00	837.50	1,416.67	1,416.67
White, nonelderly other				
Owners	633.00	833.33	1,342.08	1,608.33
Renters	592.00	555.00	866.67	991.67
Black				
Owners	917.00	866.67	1,479.17	1,332.59
Renters	500.00	585.00	677.73	791.67

housing services (P') and on disposable income (Y_D).[16] Thus for each household in the AHS, net housing expenditure ($P'Q$) and disposable income (Y_D) are estimated, and a nonlinear relationship between $P'Q/Y_D$ and Y is estimated by household type and tenure. Specifically, $Ln(P'Q/Y_D) = m/Y + b$. The resulting m and b coefficients are summarized in table B.11 for 1980.

Assisted Housing, 1973 and 1980

The Web of Urban Housing does not explicitly outline procedures for dealing with public housing and government-subsidized dwelling units, although these units have always been excluded from housing expenditure and housing service calculations. Our approach is to treat the number of units in assisted projects as a fixed characteristic of the zone in which they are located, and to incorporate recipients of Section 8 existing certificates directly into the model solution.

In 1973, the Section 8 existing program did not exist, but a significant number of households lived in assisted units. These households are excluded from the distributions of model households and dwellings and are characterized as fractional model units when calculating average market rent, average income, and average percent black in each zone. Changes in the stock of these units are not explicitly simulated, but the exogenously defined characteristics and location of assisted units do influence neigh-

---

16. See appendix A.

Appendix B

TABLE B.11
Alpha Functions, 1980
$(Ln(\alpha) = m/Y + b)$

Household Type	Northeast m	Northeast b	West m	West b
White, elderly				
Owners	440.8	−1.69	397.5	−2.05
Renters	295.3	−1.48	136.8	−1.25
White, nonelderly husband-wife				
Owners	707.6	−1.98	773.8	−2.21
Renters	529.0	−1.87	541.0	−1.79
White, nonelderly other				
Owners	707.6	−1.98	558.4	−2.02
Renters	362.6	−1.56	389.5	−1.56
Black				
Owners	707.6	−1.98	773.8	−2.21
Renters	287.8	−1.52	319.4	−1.53

borhood externalities. Table B.12 presents the characteristics of assisted units in 1973 and 1980.

For the 1973-1980 calibration, the Section 8 existing program is explicitly simulated, and one model household[17] in each metropolitan area is designated as eligible for assistance equal to the fair market rent (FMR) less 25 percent of income.[18] The household's consumption of housing services (Q) must exceed a minimum standard, defined as 75 percent of what the household could afford at an average unit price if PQ equaled the FMR.[19] Table B.13 presents the FMR and consumption minimum values for both prototypical metropolitan areas.

Income Tax Parameters, 1973-1980

Each model household bases its housing consumption decisions on after-tax income and effective housing expenditures.[20] Essential tax parameters include the value of an exemption times the number of exemptions for which a model household is eligible, the standard deduction, non-

---

17. Department of Housing and Urban Development, "Report on Section 8 Occupancy by Metro/Non-Metro as of December 31, 1980" (Washington, D.C.: U.S. Department of Housing and Urban Development, 1982).

18. J.R. Follain, Jr., *How Well Do Section 8 FMRs Match the Cost of Rental Housing?* (Washington, D.C.: The Urban Institute Press, 1975).

19. J. Yap, P. Greenstein, and R. Sadacca, *Nationwide Evaluation of the Existing Housing Program* (Washington, D.C.: The Urban Institute Press, 1978).

20. See appendix A.

TABLE B.12
ASSISTED UNITS, 1973 AND 1980

	Northeast				West			
	No. of Model Units	PQ	Y	Percent Black	No. of Model Units	PQ	Y	Percent Black
Central city	2.93	209.0	439.3	44.4	1.39	183.2	345.0	25.5
Suburbs	1.13	190.0	464.2	11.5	1.07	189.4	641.2	12.9
Central city	3.12	231.1	591.6	44.2	1.31	257.9	442.5	24.0
Suburbs	0.82	268.9	704.6	18.7	1.01	288.1	623.1	11.6

TABLE B.13
Section 8 Existing Parameters, 1980

	Northeast	West
Fair market rent	251.0	216.0
Quality minimum	140.5	134.7

housing itemized deductions, and marginal tax rates. In 1973 the value of an exemption is $750 (annually), and the standard deduction is 15 percent of gross income, but not less than $1,300 or more than $2,000. The corresponding 1980 values are $1,000 and $3,400.[21] The number of exemptions for which a model household is eligible is calculated from actual household sizes when the model households are generated. Nonhousing deductions are calculated as a percentage of before-tax income—5 percent for annual incomes less than $5,000; 12 percent for incomes between $5,000 and $15,000; and 10 percent for incomes between $15,000 and $100,000.[22] Table B.14 presents the tax brackets and corresponding marginal rates for 1973 and 1980.

Commuting Cost Parameters

Urban Institute Model households consider the time they spend commuting as one factor in their location decisions, and an hour of commuting time is assumed to be valued at half a household's wage rate.[23] Table B.15 presents hours per month of commuting time for central city and suburban residents in each prototypical metropolitan area, assuming twenty round trips per month. Table B.16 presents the proportion of income attributable to wages by household type and tenure in each metropolitan area. It is assumed that these values will not vary over time.

Parameter Calibration

The purpose of the model calibration process is to obtain values of five key behavioral parameters. Three demand parameters (γ_1, γ_2, γ_3) are estimated by repeatedly solving the model for 1973, until the model solution corresponds to actual conditions in 1973. Then, two supply parameters

---

21. From 1973 and 1980 personal income tax forms and instructions for married households filing jointly. Appropriate schedules are used for various household types.
22. Internal Revenue Service, *Statistics of Income 1973: Individual Income Tax Returns* (Washington, D.C.: U.S. Government Printing Office).
23. See appendix A.

TABLE B.14

Marginal Tax Rates, 1973 and 1980

1973		1980	
Taxable Income Bracket ($)	Marginal Rate (%)	Taxable Income Bracket ($)	Marginal Rate (%)
0-1,000	0.14	0-1,100	0.14
1,000-2,000	0.15	1,100-4,200	0.16
2,000-3,000	0.16	4,200-8,500	0.18
3,000-4,000	0.17	8,500-12,700	0.21
4,000-8,000	0.19	12,700-16,800	0.24
8,000-12,000	0.22	16,800-21,200	0.28
12,000-16,000	0.25	21,200-26,500	0.32
16,000-20,000	0.28	26,500-31,800	0.37
20,000-24,000	0.32	31,800-42,400	0.43
24,000-28,000	0.36	42,400-56,600	0.49
28,000-32,000	0.39	56,600-82,200	0.54
32,000-36,000	0.42	82,200-106,000	0.59
36,000-40,000	0.45	106,000-159,000	0.64
40,000-44,000	0.48	159,000-212,000	0.68
44,000-52,000	0.50	212,000+	
52,000-64,000	0.53		
64,000-76,000	0.55		
76,000-88,000	0.58		
88,000-100,000	0.60		
100,000+	0.65		

TABLE B.15

Commuting Hours Per Month

	Northeast	West
Central city	17.84	13.72
Suburbs	15.96	14.87

NOTE: U.S. Department of Commerce, Bureau of the Census, *Annual Housing Survey: 1975, Part A—General Housing Characteristics* (Washington, D.C.: U.S. Government Printing Office).

(β_1 and β_2) are estimated by repeatedly solving the model for the period 1973-1980 until the model solution corresponds to actual 1980 conditions. We have employed essentially the same calibration process described in *The Web of Urban Housing* for both the Northeast and the West. This section describes the calibration process and presents the resulting values of the calibrated parameters.

Appendix B

TABLE B.16
Proportion of Income Attributable to Wages

Household Type	Northeast	West
White, elderly		
Owners	0.15	0.12
Renters	0.13	0.09
White, nonelderly husband-wife		
Owners	0.87	0.85
Renters	0.88	0.88
White, nonelderly other		
Owners	0.69	0.69
Renters	0.71	0.79
Black		
Owners	0.70	0.66
Renters	0.61	0.68

Demand Calibration, 1973

The parameters γ_1, γ_2, and γ_3 measure the strength of household responses to relative prices, to zonal wealth, and to zonal racial composition. γ_1 is a measure of the degree to which a household is willing to increase or reduce its housing consumption in response to a favorable price. It can vary between zero and one, with zero indicating the maximum degree of responsiveness to price. γ_2 is a measure of household preference, other things being equal, for a zone with high average net rent per household. It serves as a proxy for households' attitudes toward the wealth of the zone in which they live. Its lower limit, zero, indicates no preference with respect to neighborhood wealth. It has no upper limit.

The parameter γ_3 measures a white household's attitude toward the racial composition of the zone in which it is located. Its lower limit, zero, indicates indifference to racial composition. The higher the γ_3, the stronger is the preference of each white household, other things being equal, for a zone in which there is a high percentage of white households.

Values of the γ parameters are estimated by allocating the 1973 distribution of model households to the 1973 distribution of model dwellings. β_1 and β_2 are set at one and zero, respectively, so that no new construction occurs and no changes in the level of housing services supplied by existing dwellings occur. In other words, supply is exogenously fixed, and household demand is the sole determinant of the model solution. Three criteria are used to compare 1973 model solutions to actual metropolitan conditions: racial composition by zone, relative price of housing services by zone, and average income by zone.

The goal of calibration is to find the parameter set that minimizes the overall deviation between the simulated values of these criteria and their actual values. Specifically, the overall deviation, or error, is calculated by (1) for each criterion, squaring the deviation between actual and simulated values in each zone, (2) adding the squared deviations across zones and taking the square root, (3) dividing by the sum of actual values across zones to yield a proportionate error term for that criterion, and (4) taking the simple average of the three proportionate error terms to yield a single, overall error term.

Mechanically, we calibrate the γ parameters by holding γ_2 and γ_3 fixed while searching over the γ_1 range in intervals of 0.2. Then γ_1 is fixed at the best value, and γ_2 and γ_3 are varied at intervals of 2.0 over the range 0–10. Finally, γ_1 is allowed to vary again at intervals of 0.1. Table B.17 presents the calibrated γ parameters and overall error terms for the Northeast and West. Table B.18 compares the best-fit solutions with actual metropolitan conditions for the three calibration criteria in both regions.

In both the Northeast and the West, the calibrated demand parameters do an extremely good job of replicating historical conditions; average error terms are only 2.3 percent for the Northeast and 0.6 percent for the West. The lowest error term achieved in previous demand calibrations was 4.7 percent.[24] Admittedly, the current implementation distinguishes only

TABLE B.17

CALIBRATED DEMAND PARAMETERS, 1973

	Northeast	West
γ_1	0.3	0.6
γ_2	2.0	6.0
γ_3	2.0	2.0
Error	0.023	0.0006

TABLE B.18

GOODNESS OF FIT, NORTHEAST AND WEST, 1973

	Proportion White Actual	Proportion White Model	Relative Price Actual	Relative Price Model	Average Income Actual	Average Income Model
Northeast						
Central city	0.826	0.853	0.960	0.976	$846	$811
Suburbs	0.970	0.952	1.034	1.020	$1,146	$1,175
West						
Central city	0.905	0.909	1.008	1.016	$964	$976
Suburbs	0.964	0.951	0.994	0.987	$1,096	$1,092

Appendix B

two zones; nevertheless, the low average error terms indicate that our enhancements to the data procedures have paid off in a relatively reliable predictive model. The difference in average error terms for the two regions stems from the fact that the model predicts relative prices better in the West than it does in the Northeast. Racial composition and average incomes are simulated extremely accurately for both regions.

Supply Calibration, 1973–1980

Once the demand parameters have been estimated, the model is repeatedly solved for the period 1973–1980 in order to estimate two housing supply parameters, β_1 and β_2. The β_1 parameter reflects the rate at which the quantity of housing services declines if no new capital inputs are added over the period. Its value can range from zero to one. A β_1 value of zero would imply that, if no capital inputs were added, the initial level of housing services offered by a model dwelling would be completely dissipated by 1980. A β_1 value of one, on the other hand, would imply that no depreciation in the level of housing services occurs over the 1973–1980 period. The β_2 parameter measures the responsiveness of housing supply to changes in prices. Its value can range from zero up, and higher β_2 values imply greater responsiveness to price.

Five criteria are used in comparing 1973–1980 model solutions with actual metropolitan conditions in 1980: racial composition by zone, average monthly housing expenditures by zone, average monthly income by zone, the proportion of the 1973 stock still in the inventory in 1980, and the mean income of new dwelling occupants.

Again, the goal of calibration is to find the parameter set that minimizes the overall deviation between simulated values of these criteria and their historical values. The technique described earlier for calculating an average overall error term for the 1973 demand calibration is applied to the 1973–1980 calibration as well. We search for the supply parameters by varying both β_1 and β_2 simultaneously at intervals of 0.1. Table B.19

TABLE B.19

CALIBRATED SUPPLY PARAMETERS, 1973–1980

	Northeast	West
β_1	0.9	0.8
β_2	0.6	0.8
Error	0.113	0.041

24. F. de Leeuw and R. Struyk, *The Web of Urban Housing*.

presents our calibrated supply parameters; Table B.20 provides further detail by comparing the best-fit solutions to actual metropolitan conditions in 1980.

Like the 1973 calibration results, these tables demonstrate excellent predictive reliability. Our error terms of 11.3 percent for the Northeast and 4.1 percent for the West are lower than any achieved in previous calibrations.

One weakness of the 1973–1980 simulations, which is not reflected in the calibration results, is that new construction is not correctly allocated between central city and suburban locations. The total volume of new construction is predicted reasonably well for both regions, but all new construction occurs in the suburbs. This suggests that, in our 1980–1987 policy simulations, we can be reasonably confident about the level of new construction predicted, but not about its location.

Simulation Data, 1980–1987

In this implementation of the Urban Institute Model, we analyze the impact of Reagan administration policies by simulating the 1980–1987 pe-

TABLE B.20

GOODNESS OF FIT—NORTHEAST AND WEST, 1980

Northeast

	Proportion White Actual	Proportion White Model	Relative Price Actual	Relative Price Model	Average Income Actual	Average Income Model
Central city	0.797	0.625	$283	$256	$1,335	$993
Suburbs	0.957	1.000	$386	$349	$1,860	$1,849

Utilization Rate Actual	Utilization Rate Model	Average New Dwelling Income Actual	Average New Dwelling Income Model
0.976	0.829	$2,131	$1,754

West

	Proportion White Actual	Proportion White Model	Relative Price Actual	Relative Price Model	Average Income Actual	Average Income Model
Central city	0.895	0.813	$366	$325	$1,613	$1,344
Suburbs	0.958	1.000	$405	$389	$1,856	$1,856

Utilization Rate Actual	Utilization Rate Model	Average New Dwelling Income Actual	Average New Dwelling Income Model
0.966	0.973	$2,156	$1,997

Appendix B

riod under alternative policy scenarios and by comparing the model outcomes to a counterfactual case representing likely policies of a second Carter administration. This section describes the procedures employed to generate the 1980-1987 data. Details of the two contrasting policy environments are presented in chapter 4.

The Housing Stock, 1980

The same process is used to generate a 1980 dwelling distribution as was used to generate the 1973 distribution: (1) using a hedonic equation, housing expenditures (PQ) are imputed for owners, assisted renters, renters paying no cash rent, and renters not reporting their rent; (2) a price deflator for each zone is calculated from the hedonic equation as the ratio of actual average rents to the location-free average; (3) a value of Q is derived for each dwelling as PQ divided by the zonal price deflator; and (4) central city and suburban dwellings are sorted on the basis of Q and are aggregated into model dwellings.

Table B.21 identifies the variables included in the 1980 rent hedonic equation and presents the estimated parameter values for each prototypical metropolitan area. Table B.22 presents the initial price deflator calculations, assuming an average price of housing services (P) of 1.0 in each prototypical metropolitan area. However, since prices have risen considerably during the 1970s, setting the average SMSA value of P equal to 1.0 in both periods would mean that the implicit units for measuring quantities of housing services (Q) would be different for our predictive simulations than they are for our calibrations. To avoid this inconsistency, we calculate the average SMSA value of P for 1980 on the basis of the observed change in prices over the 1973-1980 period. Table B.23 presents the total percentage increase in each housing service price term from 1973 to 1980.[25] These increases are then applied to our 1973 price estimates to yield 1980 estimates. Since the average market price of housing services in an SMSA (P) is equal to $o + (\rho + \tau + \mu)$, average 1980 P values for the two regional SMSAs are 1.756 for the Northeast, and 1.567 for the West. Our final zonal price deflators for 1980 are calculated relative to these average prices rather than relative to an average housing service price of 1.0.

Table B.24 presents the distribution of 1980 model dwellings by zone in each regional prototype.

Determining the Price of Housing Services

Naturally, in addition to initial 1980 prices terms, our predictive simulations require projections of the average change in prices over the 1980-

---

25. The total percentage increase from 1973 to 1980 for each price term is obtained from the same index series used to generate the *average* percentage increase for the period.

TABLE B.21

HOUSING EXPENDITURE HEDONIC SPECIFICATION, 1980

Variable	Label	Northeast	West
LNBLT	Log of structure age	0.410*	−0.0685**
LGAPT	Unit in building of 20 or more units	−0.00006	0.0604*
SFDET	Single-family detached unit	−0.0357	0.0665*
FLOORS	Number of floors	0.0176	0.0163
ELEV	Unit in building with elevator	0.0858*	0.1701*
ROOMS	Number of rooms	0.1124**	0.0639**
BEDRMS	Number of bedrooms	−0.0430*	0.0886**
NUMBTHS	Number of bathrooms	0.3069**	0.2468**
HELEC	Heating fuel is electricity	0.1936**	−0.0177
CENFURN	Unit has central furnace	0.1744**	0.0512
BADHEAT	Unit has inadequate heating equipment	−0.0593	−0.1137**
STMHEAT	Unit heated with steam	0.2342**	−0.1007*
CENAIR	Unit has central air conditioner	0.3995**	−0.0080
HOLES	Unit has holes in walls or floors	0.0676	−0.0541
CRACKS	Unit has cracks in walls or ceiling	0.0021	−0.0590
PLASTER	Unit has large areas of peeling plaster	0.0006	−0.0038
ABAN	Abandoned buildings on street	−0.1981**	−0.1528**
CENCITY	Unit located in central city	−0.1389**	0.0147
BLACK	Household head is black	−0.1606**	−0.1515**
LENGTEN	Length of tenure	−0.0107**	−0.0290**
ZCROWD	Unit overcrowded	0.1181**	0.0096
constant		4.6033**	5.3696**
R^2		0.260	0.317

NOTE: * indicates significance at the 95 percent confidence level; ** indicates significance at the 99 percent confidence level.

1987 period. Table B.25 presents the projections we have adopted for both the Reagan I and Carter II programs, as well as the resulting period-long price values. The projected increases in o and μ are based on long-term national forecasts of price deflators for household operations and residential structures. To the degree that regional price changes in the 1970s differed from national trends, the regional difference is assumed to persist in the 1980s. Similarly, the projected increase in ρ is based on long-term national forecasts by Data Resources of mortgage rates on existing homes. Property tax rates are assumed to remain constant in the 1980s. Appreciation benefits are assumed to be about half of what they were in the 1970s.

As discussed in chapter 4, prices of operations, mortgage interest, and maintenance are influenced by ERTA. Therefore, the Carter II price values are derived from pre-ERTA forecasts, and the Reagan I price values reflect post-ERTA forecasts.

The basic parameters governing new construction are assumed to remain essentially unchanged in the 1980s. Thus minimum quantities of new

TABLE B.22
Housing Expenditures and Price Deflators, 1980

	Northeast	West
SMSA average PQ	$298	$345
Central city		
PQ	$245	$323
P_k	0.9119	0.9910
Suburbs		
PQ	$277	$361
P_k	1.0763	1.0006

TABLE B.23
Housing Service Prices, 1980

	Northeast	West
o-1973 value	0.394	0.394
Percentage change, 1973–1980	131.2	100.3
1980 value	0.911	0.789
ρ-1973 value	0.244	0.244
Percentage change, 1973–1980	59.1	59.1
1980 value	0.388	0.388
τ-1973 value	0.195	0.195
Percentage change, 1973–1980	−17.4	−61.1
1980 value	0.161	0.076
μ-1973 value	0.167	0.167
Percentage change, 1973–1980	77.2	88.1
1980 value	0.296	0.314

TABLE B.24
Number of Model Dwellings by Zone, 1980

	Northeast	West
Central city	33	38
Suburbs	47	54
Total	80	92

TABLE B.25

HOUSING PRICE COMPONENTS, 1980–1987
FOR THE CARTER II AND REAGAN I PROGRAMS

	Carter II		Reagan I	
	Northeast	West	Northeast	West
o-1980 value	0.911	0.789	0.911	0.789
Percentage change,				
1980–1987 average	40.8	31.2	42.1	32.2
1980–1987 value	1.283	1.035	1.294	1.043
ρ-1980 value	0.388	0.388	0.388	0.388
Percentage change,				
1980–1987 average	−2.4	−2.4	13.1	13.1
1980–1987 value	0.379	0.379	0.433	0.433
τ-1980–1987 value	0.161	0.076	0.161	0.076
μ-1980 value	0.296	0.314	0.296	0.314
Percentage change,				
1980–1987 average	33.2	37.9	26.0	29.7
1980–1987 value	0.394	0.433	0.373	0.407
V-1980–1987 value	0.027	0.160	0.027	0.160

dwelling services are kept at their 1973–1980 values, and new construction continues to enjoy the same operating cost discount.

Population Characteristics, 1987

Projected distributions of metropolitan households in 1987 are generated in a three-step process. The first step is to estimate the total growth in numbers of metropolitan households from 1980 to 1987 for each region. These estimates are obtained by adjusting regional population changes by the national ratio of household growth relative to population growth.[26] This process yields an increase in households of 4.24 percent in the Northeast and 16.38 percent in the West. The second step is to allocate the household growth across our four household types. This is accomplished by applying national projections of the relative size of black, elderly, and husband-wife populations in 1987. Within each household type, the ratio

---

26. U.S. Bureau of the Census, *Projections of Number of Households and Families: 1975 to 1995* (Washington, D.C.: U.S. Government Printing Office, 1979), Series P-25, no. 805, table 2; and U.S. Bureau of the Census, *Projections of the Population of the U.S.: 1977–2050* (Washington, D.C.: U.S. Government Printing Office, 1977), Series P-25, no. 704, table 8.

Appendix B

of owner-occupants to renters is assumed to remain the same as in the 1970s.

Once control totals for each type and tenure category are estimated, model households are constructed from an "aged" data file, in which 1988 household composition and incomes have been simulated using the Urban Institute's TRIM Model. We classify the TRIM households by type, deflate their projected incomes back to 1987 terms, and aggregate them into model households on the basis of income. The initial set of model households generated by means of this process includes households living in assisted units. As discussed in the next section, when the characteristics of households in assisted units are determined, an appropriate number of model households is removed from the initial distribution.

Table B.26 presents the distribution of 1987 households by type and tenure; table B.27 presents the corresponding median income values. Data are not available to reestimate 1987 α functions. Therefore, we assume that the 1980 functions apply, but deflate household incomes back to 1980 terms for purposes of calculating α values.

Assisted Housing, 1987

For the Carter II data set, we assume a continuation of Carter administration housing policies throughout the 1980s: 100,000 units of assisted new construction annually and 150,000 additional units of Section 8 existing assistance annually.[27] As discussed in chapter 4, the Reagan I case

TABLE B.26

NUMBER OF MODEL HOUSEHOLDS BY TYPE AND TENURE, 1987

Household Type	Northeast	West
White, elderly		
Owners	9	9
Renters	6	5
White, nonelderly husband-wife		
Owners	29	41
Renters	10	15
White, nonelderly other		
Owners	8	12
Renters	15	21
Black		
Owners	3	2
Renters	8	6

27. As of 1980, about 400,000 units of new construction subsidy were in the pipeline. These units add to the pool of assisted units built in the 1980s. However, we can assume that a corresponding number of the units allocated between 1980 and 1987 will not have reached occupancy by 1987. Therefore, we do not explicitly include the pipeline projects.

TABLE B.27

MEDIAN MONTHLY INCOMES BY HOUSEHOLD TYPE AND TENURE, 1987
(IN 1987 DOLLARS)

Household Type	Northeast	West
White, elderly		
Owners	1,688	1,658
Renters	1,095	998
White, nonelderly husband-wife		
Owners	3,995	4,097
Renters	2,272	2,163
White, nonelderly other		
Owners	2,185	2,252
Renters	1,420	1,629
Black		
Owners	2,445	2,478
Renters	1,411	1,450

TABLE B.28

ADDITIONAL UNITS OF HOUSING ASSISTANCE, 1987, IN THE CARTER II
AND REAGAN I PROGRAMS

	Carter II		Reagan I	
	Northeast	West	Northeast	West
New construction				
Actual units	253,050	100,800	25,305	10,080
Model units	1.5	0.8	0	0
Section 8 existing				
Actual units	379,575	151,200	101,220	40,320
Model units	2	1	1	0

assumes only 10,000 units of new construction and 40,000 units of existing assistance annually. On the basis of 1980 "fair share" allocation formulas, we assign 75 percent of the new units to metropolitan areas, with 48 percent of the metropolitan units allocated to the Northeast and 19 percent allocated to the West. Table B.28 presents the total numbers of assisted units added to metropolitan areas in each region, both in terms of actual dwellings and in terms of model dwellings, for the Reagan I and Carter II programs.

The total number of assisted units in each region is obtained by adding the projected additions to the number of assisted units as of 1980. For new construction units, we assume that the 1980 distribution across house-

Appendix B

hold types and zones persists. This assumption then allows us to remove model households from the initial distribution, exogenously allocating them to assisted projects.

The model households removed from the initial distribution are selected at random from the two lowest income quintiles. Section 8 existing units are not eliminated from the distribution of model households, since they participate in the market solution.